Collir
LITTLE BOO

G000240929

IRISH
CASTLES

Orna Mulcahy

HarperCollins Publishers
Westerhill Road
Bishopbriggs
Glasgow
G64 2QT

First Edition 2020

10 9 8 7 6 5 4 3 2 1

© HarperCollins Publishers 2020

ISBN 978-0-00-834822-9

Collins® is a registered trademark
of HarperCollins Publishers Limited

www.collins.co.uk

A catalogue record for this book is
available from the British Library

Author: Orna Mulcahy

Typeset by
Davidson Publishing Solutions

Printed and bound in China by
RR Donnelley APS Co Ltd

Contents

Introduction

There's a special romance to Irish castles, whether it's the ruined stronghold of an ancient Irish clan perched on a rocky clifftop, the monumental tower rising inside a town's medieval walls, or the castellated fancy of a Victorian tycoon reflected in its own glassy lake.

Combined with the country's dramatic scenery of craggy coastline, rolling green countryside, ancient woodlands, and loughs, Ireland's most famous castles are set in dreamy locations beloved by generations of tourists, film-makers, and brides. Think of the majesty of ruined Dunluce, etched against the sky on the north Antrim coast; the thrilling bulk of Blarney Castle, home to the Blarney Stone, which is said to give those who kiss it the gift of fluent talk; or the splendour of Ashford Castle in Cong, County Mayo, the setting for film director John Ford's sentimental tribute to Ireland, *The Quiet Man*, starring John Wayne.

It's not known exactly how many castles dot the island of Ireland but it's likely to be in thousands. A high number of fortifications reflect a rebellious history reaching back to the twelfth century and lasting all the way to the 1920s, when many of Ireland's aristocratic homes were abandoned or burned during the War of Independence.

Ruins abound: fortresses destroyed by cannon fire tell of Cromwell's rampage through Ireland in the late 1640s; the shells of once grand castles, built in prosperous times and then abandoned.

This book provides a guide to 140 or so Irish castles and strongholds, many of them dating back to Norman times and earlier, some of them far more recent, but all selected for their historical or architectural significance.

Some are ancient monuments, standing strong after nearly a thousand years; others mere piles of stones in once strategic settings. Many, like grand Malahide Castle on the outskirts of Dublin and Dublin Castle in the centre of the capital, have been carefully restored and are open to the public. Others can only be viewed externally and from a distance. One or two are twentieth-century replica castles, such as Doonbeg on the County Clare coast – now owned by US President Donald Trump.

Castles first appeared in Ireland with the arrival of the Anglo-Normans in the twelfth century. Land distributed by King Henry II of England was parcelled out to royalists who built fortified towers to protect themselves from the native clans. These castles were built in strategic positions, and consisted of a large square or rectangular tower, known as a keep, surrounded by a large curtain wall. Other defensive measures were a moat, portcullis and drawbridge, and battlements.

By the beginning of the thirteenth century, stone castles began to appear, many built on the orders of King John. Amongst the earliest of these is Dublin Castle, built in 1204. The fortifications of Carrickfergus in Antrim and Trim in County Meath (once known as the Royal County) also date from this period. By the middle of the century, castles had spread throughout Ireland, built by Anglo-Norman families, who quickly integrated themselves, marrying into native families and becoming *Hiberniores Hibernis ipsis*, meaning "more Irish than the Irish themselves".

From 1400 onwards, native Irish chiefs began to build their own castles, adopting the tower house design, with battlements offering commanding views of their territories.

In 1429, Henry VI, King of England (and Lord of Ireland) granted ten pounds to any of his subjects who built a small defensive tower in the area surrounding Dublin – called The Pale – which included the counties of Meath, Louth, and Kildare. This resulted in a proliferation of "ten pound" castles of a fairly basic design, many of which survive today.

The Irish Rebellion of 1641 and the Confederate Wars that followed set the native Irish and old English Catholics against English Protestants and Scots Presbyterian planters in a bloody conflict through the land that saw castles seized and their occupants murdered. Cromwell's invasion of Ireland in 1649, and subsequent conquest, quelled the rebellion with a swathe of violent conquests through the land that left many of Ireland's castles either destroyed or confiscated and given to "planters" loyal to the English monarchy.

The 1700s saw a revival in building, with a move from the fortified tower to a more domestic style in architecture. Earlier castles were either incorporated into new country house designs or sometimes left at a distance from the new structure.

Throughout the eighteenth and particularly in the nineteenth century, many such properties were extended again, or replaced entirely, this time with the help of fortunes built in the great industrial cities of England or further afield.

The Victorian Irish had a penchant for castles, and this produced a proliferation of battlements, towers, and turrets added to homes originally built in the plain Irish Georgian style. Brand-new castles were built in the romantic style, from Kylemore Abbey in Connemara to the dramatic Glenveagh Castle in County Donegal.

But in the aftermath of the Irish Famine many estates were sold or broken up. The 1920s brought a further wave of unrest, with several great Irish homes being burned out by rebels during Ireland's War of Independence.

Many of the castles featured in this book are open to visitors. Some operate as hotels or guest houses, while others can be viewed by appointment or on certain open days of the year. However some remain privately owned and their inclusion in this book does not imply a right of public access. It is always advisable to check with the specific attraction in advance. Telephone number and website, where available, are listed in the property description.

About the author

Orna Mulcahy is a journalist and editor, who has spent much of her career writing on Irish houses and historic buildings for *The Irish Times*.

Northern Ireland

Numbers in **bold** indicate the page
where the property can be found

*Atlantic
Ocean*

Doe Castle **82**

Glenveagh Castle **106**

Mongavlin Castle **175**

N

Donegal Castle **84**

Classiebawn Castle **74**

Tully Castle **220**

Augher Castle **26**

Monea Castle **174**

Manorhamilton Castle **160**

Parkes Castle **195**

Markree Castle **161**

Crom Castle **78**

Ireland

Moygara
Castle **178**

McDermott's Castle **166**

Clogh Oughter **76**

Dunluce Castle **100**

Kinbane Castle **136**

Scotland

Dungiven Castle **97**

Kilwaughter Castle **135**

North

Channel

Shane's Castle **206**

Carrickfergus Castle **58**

thern Ireland

Killymoon Castle **134**

Belfast Castle **44**

Helen's Tower **111**

Hillsborough Castle **112**

Portaferry Castle **196**

Quintin Castle **200**

Gosford Castle **109**

Tandragee Castle **216**

Kilclief Castle **128**

Jordans Castle **122**

Hope Castle **113**

Narrow Water Castle **182**

Irish Sea **9**

Carlingford Castle **56**

West Central Ireland

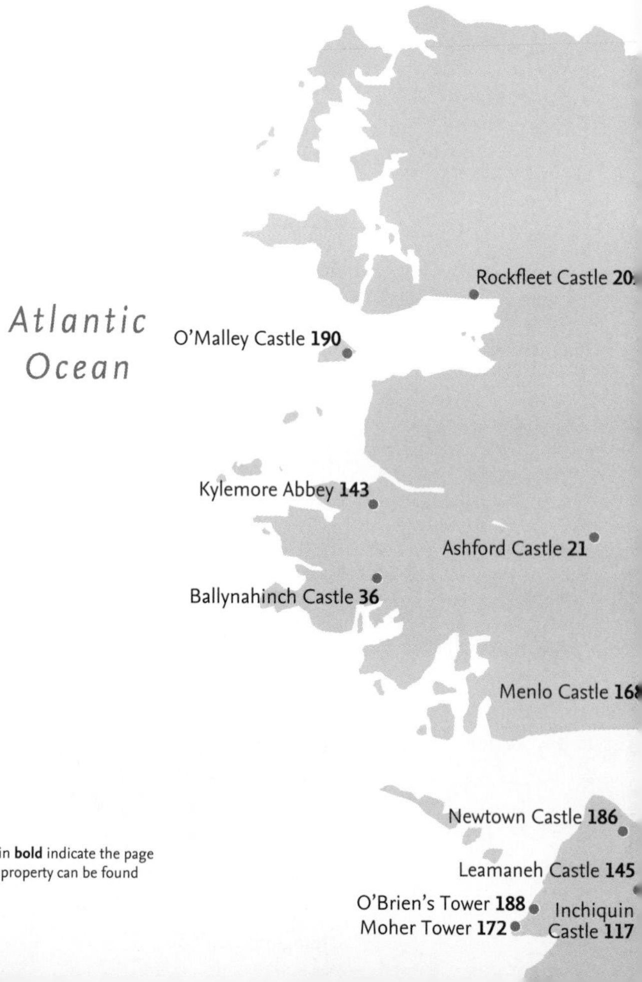

Atlantic Ocean
Rockfleet Castle 20
O'Malley Castle 190
Kylemore Abbey 143
Ashford Castle 21
Ballynahinch Castle 36
Menlo Castle 16
Newtown Castle 186
Leamaneh Castle 145
O'Brien's Tower 188
Moher Tower 172
Inchiquin Castle 117

Numbers in **bold** indicate the page where the property can be found

Monea Castle **174**

Manorhamilton Castle **160**

Parkes Castle **195**

Crom Castle **78**

Markree Castle **161**

Moygara
Castle **178**

McDermott's Castle **166**

Clogh Oughter **76**

Ballintober Castle **32**

Tullynally Castle **222**

Ireland

Knockdrin Castle **142**

Castle Hackett **66**

Lynch's
Castle **152**

Athenry Castle **24**

Moyode Castle **179**

Oranmore
Castle **192**

Ballydonnellan Castle **34**

Redwood Castle **201**

Dunguaire
Castle **98**

Isert Kelly Castle **118**

Birr Castle **46**

Leap Castle **146**

Dunamase Castle **94**

Portumna Castle **198**

Dysert O'Dea Castle **104**

Roscrea Castle **204**

11

Southwestern Ireland

Atlantic Ocean

Carrigaholt Castle **62**

Carrigafoyle Castle **60**

Glin Castle **10**

Minard Castle **170**

Drishane Castle **8**

Muckross House **180**

An Culu **16**

Dromore Castle **90**

Ballinacarriga Castle **29**

Dunboy Castle and Puxley Manor **95**

Numbers in **bold** indicate the page where the property can be found

12

Knappogue Castle 140

Nenagh Castle 184

Dromoland Castle 89

Bunratty Castle 52

King John's Castle 138

Castlegarde Castle 70

Maudlin Castle 162

Kilkenny Castle 131

keaton Castle 22

Castle Matrix 68

Thomastown Castle 217

Kilcash Castle 126

Ireland

Cahir Castle 55

Burncourt Castle 54

Ormond Castle 194

Kanturk Castle 124

Kilcolman Castle 130

Castle Pook 69

Blackwater Castle 47

Lismore Castle 147

Lohort Castle 148

Mallow Castle 156

Strancally Castle 214

Dungarvan Castle 96

Blarney Castle 48

Ardo Castle 20

Macroom Castle 154

Barryscourt Castle 42

Ballea Castle 28

Castle Bernard 64

Desmond Castle 80

Celtic Sea

East Central Ireland

Portaferry Castle **196** Quintin Castle **200**

Gosford Castle **109** Tandragee Castle **216**

Kilclief Castle **12?**

Jordans Castle **12?**

Northern Ireland

Hope Castle **113**

Narrow Water Castle **182**

Carlingford Castle **56**

Ireland Hatch's Castle **110**

Smarmore Castle **212** Barmeath Castle **40**

Irish Sea

Killua Castle **133** Slane Castle **210**

Ballinlough Castle **30** Ardgillan Castle **18**

Killeen Castle **132**

Trim Castle **218** Dunsany Castle **102** Lambay Castle **144**

Dangan Castle **79**

Malahide Castle **155**

Maynooth Castle **164** Luttrellstown Castle **150** Howth Castle **114**

Castletown House **72** Clontarf Castle **77**

Drimnagh Castle **86** Dublin Castle **92**

Monkstown Castle **176** Bulloch Castle **50**

Manderley Castle **158**

Jigginstown Castle **119**

Barretstown Castle **41**

Luggala Lodge **149**

Monkstown Castle **176**

Bulloch Castle **50**

Manderley Castle **158**

Jigginstown Castle **119**

Barretstown Castle **41**

Luggala Lodge **149**

Ireland

Carnew Castle **57**

Huntington Castle **116**

Irish Sea

Mountgarrett Castle **177**

Ballyhack Castle **35**

Johnstown Castle **120**

Waterford Castle **223**

Bargy Castle **38**

Slade Castle **208**

Celtic Sea

Numbers in **bold** indicate the page
where the property can be found

An Culu

A picture-perfect castle overlooking Kenmare Bay, An Culu looks like a particularly well preserved medieval castle or, at the least, a Victorian Gothic revival masterpiece, but in fact it dates from the 1990s, when it was built by an English businessman smitten with history. The first castle to be built in Ireland since Victorian times, it comes with all the architectural detail one might expect: a moat and a drawbridge, turrets and towers, a grotto-style swimming pool in the dungeon, and gas-fired torches that can be activated by remote control in the entrance. An Culu took three years to build, using teams of craftsmen from all over Ireland and the UK, as well as local stonemasons and joiners. It's surrounded by forest managed by the Irish Forestry Board, Coillte.

An Culu is privately owned and cannot be visited.

Ardgillan Castle

STRIFELAND, BALBRIGGAN, COUNTY DUBLIN
+353 1 849 2212 | *www.ardgillancastle.ie*

Dating from 1738 and with considerable embellishment in the 1800s, Ardgillan Castle sits in a parkland setting in North County Dublin, with views over the sea. Ardgillan was originally built as a large country house, and the castellations were added in the 1800s. It was built by the Taylor family, whose ancestor Thomas Taylor had moved to Ireland from England in 1660 to be the Chief Examiner of the Down Survey of Ireland, the first detailed national land survey in the world. This survey was necessary after Cromwell's Irish campaigns, which ended much land ownership for Catholics, providing opportunities for Protestants such as Taylor, who was able to buy up over 20,000 acres in Ireland. The Taylor family owned the property for over two centuries, but it is now owned by the State and is open to the public all year round for tours, refreshments, and activities. It sits in 194 acres of grassland and woodland, including walled, ornamental, and rose gardens.

Ardo Castle

ARDOGINNA, COUNTY WATERFORD
www.ardmorewaterford.com

Ruined and romantic, Ardo Castle stands on a clifftop, looking out to sea, near the pretty seaside village of Ardmore in County Waterford. Dating from the seventeenth century, its eclectic collection of towers, walls, gates, and turrets matches its string of owners and their fortunes. The first owner mentioned was a Fitzgerald, of Norman stock, whose heir, it is said, was caught stealing a gold cup and hanged. In the eighteenth century, the castle was owned by a Jeremiah Coughlan, whose wife is said to have supported her extravagant lifestyle by helping local smugglers. The ownership passed to Marshal McMahon who was President and Marshal of France in 1873. Finally, the castle was purchased by the McKenna family, who lived in it for some years until the end of the First World War, after which it was abandoned.

Ashford Castle

ASHFORD CASTLE ESTATE, CONG, COUNTY MAYO, F31 CA48
+353 94 954 6003

An awe-inducing baronial castle on Lough Corrib, close to the village of Cong, Ashford Castle was once owned by the Guinness brewing family and is now a luxury hotel with a plush, romantic interior. The earliest segment of the castle dates back to the early thirteenth century, when it was built on the edge of a monastic settlement by the de Burgo family. Defeated in battle in 1589, they lost their home to Lord Ingham, Governor of Connaught, whose family held it for over three hundred years. It was not until 1715, when the castle was acquired by the Browne family, that it became the Ashford estate, with the castle extended in the French chateau style. The castellated wings and the bridge entrance were added by the Guinness family, who acquired Ashford in the mid nineteenth century and extended the estate to 26,000 acres.

Askeaton Castle

HIGH STREET, CROOM, COUNTY LIMERICK
www.limerick.ie

Askeaton Castle stands on a small island in the river Deel in County Limerick. Started in 1199 and now a ruin, it was one of the castles of the Fitzgeralds, the Earls of Desmond, who arrived with the Norman invasion but who adopted the local language, laws, and culture to become "more Irish than the Irish themselves", it was said. The Fitzgeralds ruled Munster from this castle for several centuries, until the English forces ate away at their support and drove them out in the late 1500s. The castle was destroyed by the forces of Cromwell in 1652, when it was defended by confederate Catholic forces.

The castle has a fine banqueting hall, with interesting architectural windows built above wine cellars and kitchens, testament to the importance of entertaining to the Irish nobility. Close by are two other ruins of interest: a fourteenth-century Franciscan friary founded by the Fitzgeralds, destroyed by an English commander in 1579 after failing to take the castle itself, and the 1740 Hellfire Club, where rich men were said to have gathered for entertainments and excesses of various kinds.

Athenry Castle

GORTEENACRA, ATHENRY, COUNTY GALWAY
+353 91 844 797 | *www.athenryheritagecentre.com*

This is a fine restored thirteenth-century castle in the medieval walled town of Athenry, about fifteen miles from the city of Galway. The castle was built by the Anglo-Norman lord, Meyler de Bermingham, c. 1237, after he was granted lands following the Conquest of Connaught. Having built an imposing tower surrounded by defensive walls, he then set about developing the town, adding a parish church, a priory, a hospital, streets, houses, and a marketplace. By the end of the thirteenth century, Athenry was a wealthy and important market town with trading links to England and the Continent. Town walls were built in 1316 to protect the inhabitants from the warring Irish, but over the next two centuries the town declined.

Augher Castle

also known as SPUR ROYAL CASTLE, AUGHER,
COUNTY TYRONE

Augher Castle is a tower house built around 1615 by
Thomas Ridgeway, a Devon man who served as Treasurer
of Ireland and who assisted in the Plantation of Ulster.
For this he was awarded 2000 acres of land in County
Tyrone and later a title, the Earl of Londonderry. He built
Augher Castle on the site of an older fortress but he
didn't spend much time there, and political ambitions
found him often in London. Augher Castle was burned
in 1689 by the Jacobites as the Siege of Derry was under
way. It was originally a square, three-storey Plantation
castle, with an unusual triangular tower in the middle of
each of its sides. The castle was restored around 1832 by
Sir James Richardson-Bunbury, who added two
castellated wings, transforming the old castle into a
Georgian mansion house. The house remains in the
Richardson-Bunbury family today.

Ballea Castle

CARRIGALINE, COUNTY CORK

Situated on a cliff overlooking the Owenboy river in Carrigaline, south of Cork City, Ballea dates from the fifteenth century, when it was home to the McCarthy family. Extended in the seventeenth century by the McCarthys, the castle eventually fell into disrepair until around 1750, when restoration work was undertaken by the Hodder family, who owned Ballea until the early 1900s. The castle has been modernized in more recent times and is now a private residence.

Ballinacarriga Castle

DUNMANWAY, WEST CORK

Situated on a high rocky outcrop overlooking Ballinacarriga Lough in West Cork, Ballinacarriga tower house is believed to have been built by the O'Muirthile (Hurley) family, with the date 1585 carved into the wall on the fourth floor. But there is evidence that the castle was originally an older McCarthy stronghold. Inside, at the second-storey level, carving in the window embrasure is of a female figure accompanied by five roses, thought to be of Catherine O'Cullane, wife of Randall Hurley, and her five children. The castle and lands were confiscated and granted to English settlers after the family joined the rebellion of 1641 against the English settlement of Munster. The castle passed through various families and some religious carvings suggest it may also have been used as a church. It has been unoccupied since the early nineteenth century.

Ballinlough Castle

CLONMELLON, COUNTY WESTMEATH
+353 46 943 3234 | *www.ballinloughcastle.ie*

Built in 1641, Ballinlough is the ancestral home of the Nugent family, who claim lineage back to Brian, the fourth king of Connacht. Legend goes that he had one daughter and 24 sons, twelve of whom are said to have been baptized by St Patrick. The coat of arms over the front door is that of the O'Reilly clan: the family changed their name from O'Reilly to Nugent to avail of a dowry in 1812. Since then several generations of Baronet Nugents have occupied the house, making them one of the very few seventeenth-century Irish Catholic families who still live in their original family home. The castle was extended in the late eighteenth century, when a new wing was added to the design of the talented amateur architect Thomas Wogan Browne, who was responsible for Malahide Castle on the outskirts of Dublin. Today Ballinlough is best known as the venue for the popular Body & Soul festival which takes place in the grounds in the month of June. The house is also available as a venue for weddings and events, and the extensive grounds are also open to the public.

Ballintober Castle

BALLINTOBER, COUNTY ROSCOMMON
www.roscommon.ie

A large moated castle with a central courtyard, or bawn, of 1.5 acres, Ballintober dates from around 1290. It was built on an imposing scale, with enormous corner towers and small projecting turrets. It is thought the builder was William de Burgo, and that the castle's large area was intended to permit an Anglo-Norman settlement within its walls but, within a few decades of being built, Ballintober came into the possession of the O'Connor clan and was the seat of the O'Connor Don until 1652. In 1598, the castle was taken by Red Hugh O'Donnell, who used cannons to bombard it and forced Hugh O'Connor Don to renounce his allegiance to the Crown. In 1641, it became a centre of Catholic resistance and it was confiscated in 1652. The castle and lands were restored to the O'Connors in 1677 and they remained there until 1701, when the castle was abandoned and fell into ruin.

Ballydonnellan Castle

LOUGHREA, COUNTY GALWAY

All that remains today of the stronghold of the powerful
O'Donnellan clan, who controlled lands between Lough
Rea and Ballinsloe, is a ruin of a fifteenth-century tower
and the substantial house grafted onto it in the mid
eighteenth century. Ballydonnellan Castle is likely to
have been built some time after 1412, an early fortress
on the site having been destroyed by fire. The entire
edifice was still standing when it was mapped in the
1890s, but had fallen into decay by the early twentieth
century and is now in ruins. Fragments of its former
glory, such as fine plasterwork, can be glimpsed through
the ivy that has all but engulfed it.

Ballyhack Castle

BALLYHACK, COUNTY WEXFORD

+353 51 389468 | *www.heritageireland.ie*

A well-preserved fifteenth-century tower house that stands guard over the Waterford Estuary, Ballyhack Castle is thought to have been built, circa 1450, by the Order of Knights of the Hospital of Saint John of Jerusalem, a military order founded at the beginning of the twelfth century at the time of the Crusades. The castle is open to the public, having been partially restored, and visitors can see a classic murder hole that allowed for attackers to be assaulted from above with cascade of rocks. A permanent exhibition displays objects relating to the Crusades, the Normans, and medieval monks.

Ballynahinch Castle

RECESS, CONNEMARA, COUNTY GALWAY
+353 95 31006 | *www.ballynahinch-castle.com*

Surrounded by woodlands in the heart of Connemara
with a backdrop of the Twelve Bens mountains,
Ballynahinch Castle was built in the eighteenth century
by the powerful Martin family, who produced Humanity
Dick Martin, an MP so named for his championing of
animal rights, but also known as Hair-Trigger Dick for
the several people he killed or wounded in duels.

The castle is set on the banks of the Owenmore river,
renowned for its fly fishing, and it was this that attracted
the Indian prince and cricketer Ranjitsinhji ("Ranji"), who
fell for its romantic setting in the 1920s. He renovated
the castle and built fishing huts and piers along the river,
and he lived at Ballynahinch until his death in 1933.
The castle has been run as an up-market hotel since
1946 and has recently been entirely refurbished by its
current owner, the businessman Denis O'Brien.

Bargy Castle

One of a number of fortresses built in the fifteenth century by the Rossiter family who settled in Ireland following the Norman invasion, Bargy Castle was confiscated by Cromwell in 1667, in response to Rossiter's part in the defence of Wexford. The castle was then granted to William Ivory, who sold it to the Harvey family. They held it until the mid twentieth century, when it was bought by General Sir Eric de Burgh, a former Chief of Staff in the Indian Army, and the grandfather of musician and songwriter Chris de Burgh. The singer lived there as a child with his parents Charles and Maeve Davison, who ran the castle as a hotel.

The castle is a private residence and cannot be visited.

Barmeath Castle

DUNLEER, COUNTY LOUTH

+353 41 685 1205 | *www.barmeath-castle.com*

Originally the site of a medieval tower house with sweeping views over Dundalk Bay, Barmeath Castle was enlarged in the mid eighteenth century, with the addition of a substantial residence that has been home to the Bellew family for generations. The impressive castellated façade was enhanced in the 1830s with the addition of a portcullis entrance, and a turreted curtain wall that encloses a large courtyard. The castle is surrounded by ten acres of the gardens originally laid out by English landscape architect and astronomer Thomas Wright. The gardens, which have been restored in recent years, include an eighteenth-century archery ground surrounded by Irish yew.

The castle is available to rent on Airbnb.

Barretstown Castle

BALLYMORE EUSTACE, COUNTY KILDARE

+353 45 864 115 | *www.barretstown.org*

A tower house with a Gothic Victorian addition, Barretstown was first recorded in a 1547 inquisition held after the Dissolution of the Monasteries, when it was listed as the property of the Archbishop of Dublin. It was confiscated by the Crown and subsequently leased to the Eustaces, a distinguished family who had arrived in Ireland at the time of the Norman invasion and who gave their name to the town that grew up around it – Ballymore Eustace. The castle has had a number of wealthy international owners including cosmetics tycoon Elizabeth Arden and billionaire retailer Galen Weston, who gifted it to the Irish State. Since the mid 1990s, the 500-acre estate has been run as a camp and respite centre for seriously ill children and their families, by a charity founded by the late actor Paul Newman.

41

Barryscourt Castle

A typical fifteenth-century tower house, Barryscourt Castle was for centuries home to the Norman De Barry family. There is evidence that this site has been occupied for as long as one thousand years. Phillip De Barry built a castle here in 1202, but the present tower dates from around the mid sixteenth century.

Belfast Castle

ANTRIM ROAD, BELFAST, BT15 5GR
+44 28 9077 6925 | *www.belfastcastle.co.uk*

The original Belfast Castle, built in the late twelfth century by the Normans, was located in the heart of the city, around Castle Place and Donegall Place. It was the stronghold of the first Baron Chichester (better known as Sir Arthur Chichester), but was burned down in 1708, leaving only street names to mark the site. The Chichester family decamped to the suburbs and today's Belfast Castle was built in the mid nineteenth century by the third Marquess of Donegall, who designed it in the Scottish baronial style. The castle cost a fortune to build, and was designed by Charles Lanyon of the architectural firm Lanyon, Lynn and Lanyon. After Lord Donegall's death and the family's financial demise, the eighth Earl of Shaftesbury, who had married into the family, completed the castle, which was subsequently presented to the city of Belfast. It is now used for civic functions and private events but it does have an interesting visitor centre telling the story of the surrounding area from Stone Age times. The grounds also include an adventure playground for children.

Birr Castle

TOWNPARKS, BIRR, COUNTY OFFALY
+353 57 912 0336 | *www.birrcastle.com*

In 1620, Sir Laurence Parsons built a new castle on
the site of an older building, and then extensively
refurbished it in the 1640s. The nineteenth century saw
Birr become a great centre of scientific research, when
William Parsons, the third Earl, built a great telescope in
the grounds. His wife Mary, whose fortune helped him
to build the telescope and make many improvements to
the castle, was a keen photographer. Her perfectly
preserved dark room is one of the many fascinating
aspects of the castle's superbly decorated interior. The
castle grounds are open to the public and have been
enhanced to include a Science Centre.

Birr Castle remains the private residence of the
Parsons family.

Blackwater Castle

CASTLETOWNROCHE, COUNTY CORK
+353 22 26333 | *www.blackwatercastle.com*

Held by just two families over the course of eight hundred years, Blackwater Castle has retained many of its historical features, which can be seen today, as the house is open to the public for guided tours, events, and overnight stays. The earliest parts of the castle date from the twelfth century, when it came into the possession of the powerful Roche family, who lived there for half a millennium. It later passed to the Widenham family, who renamed it Castle Widenham and occupied it until the 1960s. The castle and surrounding lands contain evidence of Mesolithic occupation and early Iron Age settlement, with evidence of ring forts in the immediate area, a St Patrick's Holy Well, medieval defence walls, a thirteenth-century watch tower and sentry walk and a fifteenth-century Norman keep.

Blarney Castle

BLARNEY, COUNTY CORK
+353 21 438 5252 | *info@blarneycastle.ie*

A world-famous tourist attraction because of the Blarney Stone built into its battlements, Blarney Castle dates from 1446, when it was built by the McCarthys of Muskerry on a rocky outcrop with commanding views of the surrounding countryside. The vast keep was eventually acquired by the St John Jefferyes family, who built a Gothic-style Georgian house alongside it. This house subsequently burned down, its ruins now forming part of the property, which also includes a landscaped garden known as Rock Close, filled with dolmen-type stones arranged to look as if they had been standing since prehistoric times. The castle is most famous for its Blarney Stone, which, when kissed, is supposed to confer the gift of the gab. The association with the name Blarney dates back to when an early McCarthy owner tried to talk his way out of handing over Blarney Castle to an agent of Queen Elizabeth, who is said to have declared, 'I will have no more of this Blarney talk!'

Bullock Castle

DALKEY, COUNTY DUBLIN

Dating from the twelfth century, Bullock Castle was built on land given to Cistercian monks, along with valuable fishing rights in the busy harbour. To protect these rights, the castle was built, and a small village grew up around it. Primarily built for defence, Bullock Castle was also used as an inn for the cross-channel traffic, and the monks were known far and wide for their hospitality and for the taxes they exacted from every fishing boat entering the harbour that had to be paid in fish. In 1346, the fishermen brought action against the Abbot for taking some of their catch, but the monks won the case.

Today the castle lies rather incongruously within the grounds of a nursing home, Our Lady's Manor, a short stroll away from Bullock harbour, where a family of seals regularly appear, and where you can also buy fresh fish from the boats that head out each day to tend their lobster pots. Dalkey village itself is a ten-minute walk away, and here you will find plenty of cafes and restaurants and some notable pubs, including Finnegan's on Sorrento Road, which is Bono's local.

Bunratty Castle & Folk Park

Standing proud above the Shannon Estuary, Bunratty Castle in County Clare dates from the early 1400s, though there had been a settlement on the site from the thirteenth century. The castle came into the possession of the O'Brien family, who became Earls of Thomond and lived in splendour in the vast tower house before succumbing to Cromwell's forces. By the end of the nineteenth century the castle had been abandoned, the ceiling of its great hall collapsed. However, in the early 1950s it was rescued by Viscount Gort, a medievalist who bought Bunratty for a nominal sum and set about restoring the castle with the help of the Irish government and the art collector, John Hunt. The Gorts and Hunt furnished the castle with a valuable collection of early furniture and works of art, to recreate the lifestyle of the O'Briens. Today, the castle welcomes thousands of visitors daily, and hosts the renowned Bunratty Medieval Banquet in the great hall, with staff dressed in medieval costumes, and Irish mead (a honey concoction) served with dinner.

Burncourt Castle

CLOGHEEN, COUNTY TIPPERARY

Did ever a castle have so short a life as Burncourt? The tower house was built on lands granted to Sir Richard Everard by Charles I in 1639 and completed in 1641. Sir Richard joined the Catholic Confederates at Kilkenny in 1642 and thus became a marked man. His castle was destroyed by fire in 1650. Some reports say it was burned down by Oliver Cromwell's troops, others say the Everard family burned it themselves to prevent the troops capturing the castle. This gave rise to a rhyme: "It was seven years in building, seven years in living and fifteen days in burning." The castle was destroyed, and Sir Richard Everard, who was involved in defending the city of Limerick against Cromwell's troops, was captured and hanged by Cromwell's son-in-law, General Ireton, in 1651.

Cahir Castle

CASTLE STREET, CAHIR, COUNTY TIPPERARY, E21 P652
+353 52 744 1011 | *www.heritageireland.ie*

Ancient seat of the Butlers, who became the Earls of Glengall, Cahir Castle is situated on an island in the river Suir in the town of Cahir, with its own parkland stretching behind it. Dating from the fifteenth century, it's among the best preserved castles in Ireland, despite an embattled history that saw it ransacked by the Earl of Essex and Cromwell's men. The castle consists of three courtyards, known as wards, with the central building in the inner ward. The family moved out of the castle in the eighteenth century and built an impressive house in the village. The first Earl of Glengall had also built, around 1810, a Swiss Cottage in the castle's grounds to accommodate guests. Cahir Castle is thought to have been designed by John Nash, with a lavishly decorated interior and a thatched roof.

Carlingford Castle

CARLINGFORD, COUNTY LOUTH

+353 42 937 3454 | *www.carlingford.ie*

This dramatic fortress was strategically built on the shores of Carlingford Lough around 1200 by Hugh de Lacy, Lord of Meath, shortly after the Norman invasion of Ireland. The walled enclosure, which housed two rectangular towers, acquired the name "King John's Castle", after King John, Lord of Ireland, supposedly stayed there for three days in 1210, during an expedition to Ireland when he invaded Ulster. It's said that the king began to draft the Magna Carta (agreed in 1215) at Carlingford, but records show that he also commissioned men and materials to extend the castle itself. The castle appears to have remained in English hands during the post-medieval period, but was subject to many attacks and subsequently taken by new owners in 1596, 1642, 1649 and 1650. It is now in ruins.

Carnew Castle

CARNEW, COUNTY WICKLOW

Set behind a high castellated wall in the middle of the
pretty village of Carnew, this tower house was built in
the late sixteenth century. Battered by Cromwell's troops,
it was mostly in ruins by the end of the eighteenth
century, but its fortunes revived in 1817, when the fourth
Earl of Fitzwilliam repaired and modernized the castle in
Gothic Georgian style. It became a rectory later in the
nineteenth century. Now a private home, it continues to
crumble, with parts of its boundary wall having collapsed
into a village street.

Carrickfergus Castle

MARINE HIGHWAY, CARRICKFERGUS, BT38 7BG

+44 028 9335 1273 | *www.midandeastantrim.gov.uk/
tourism/things-to-do/carrickfergus-castle*

Occupying a commanding position overlooking Belfast
Lough, Carrickfergus Castle was long considered Ulster's
most important garrison. It dates from the early years of
the twelfth century, when it was built by John de Courcy,
after he conquered the east of Ulster and ruled as a petty
king. Later he was ousted by another Norman invader,
Hugh de Lacy, who added substantially to the castle,
building a bailey at the end of the pier, with a high
curtain wall and east gate. For centuries the castle
withstood waves of invasion, fending off the Scots, Irish,
English, and French, and often being used as a prison.
Its heavy fortifications ensured its central role in military
manoeuvres until 1928, when it was acquired by the
British government. During the First World War it was
used as a garrison and ordnance store and during the
Second World War as an air-raid shelter. Today it is
maintained by Northern Ireland Environment Agency,
and has been fully restored with a permanent exhibition
of life in medieval times.

Carrigafoyle Castle

CARRIGAFOYLE, BALLYLONGFORD, COUNTY KERRY
+353 68 43304

Once considered the "Guardian of the Shannon" because of its strategic location overlooking the shipping lanes running in and out of the city of Limerick, Carrigafoyle Castle was most likely built in the 1490s by Conor Liath O'Connor, and took its name from the Irish Carraig an Phoill, meaning "rock of the hole". The five-storey castle has an unusual wide spiral staircase of 104 steps leading to the battlements. Also unusual is the "pigeon room", in which birds were kept for food. It came under attack by English forces in 1580, and succumbed after a two-day battle in which all the inhabitants, including Spanish soldiers, were either killed or were hanged shortly afterwards. The castle, which was never repaired, can be visited today.

Carrigaholt Castle

CARRIGAHOLT, COUNTY CLARE
www.loophead.ie/carrigaholt-castle

Strategically located overlooking the Shannon Estuary on the Loop Head peninsula, Carrigaholt Castle is a traditional tower house built around 1480 by the McMahon family. It was occupied by Teige Caech "the short-sighted" McMahon in September 1588, when seven ships from the Spanish Armada anchored in the estuary. Even though the McMahons offered no aid to the Spanish, the tower house was attacked by Sir Conyers Clifford, the Governor of Connaught. The following year the castle was captured by the Earl of Thomond, Donagh O'Brien. The final siege of the castle took place in 1649, when it was taken by General Ludlow. The last McMahon in residence was Teige Keigh, before the castle was granted to Henry O'Brien by Queen Elizabeth. The castle continued to be inhabited until the late nineteenth century, when the last owners, the Burton family, finally quit.

The castle is now in ruins, and it is not possible to visit.

Castle Bernard

A ruined castle that was once the seat of the O'Mahony clan, and originally called Castle Mahon, it was acquired by the Bernard family in the early seventeenth century, and added to in several phases over the next two hundred years by the Earls of Bandon. James Francis Bernard, the 4th Earl of Bandon (1850–1924), was a British Deputy Lieutenant in Ireland and a Representative Peer. During the War of Independence, the house was burned down by the IRA, who then kidnapped James Francis Bernard and held him in captivity for three weeks, though it's said he got on tolerably well with his captors, with whom he played cards. The title died with the last Earl of Bandon in 1979 and after his wife's death the house was inherited by their daughter, Jennifer, who left her career at John Lewis in London to manage the 400-acre estate on the banks of the river Bandon. On summer evenings she liked to entertain guests in the dungeon of the old castle, which is now out of bounds. After her death, Castle Bernard passed to her sister, and it remains a private residence.

Castle Hackett

Now an ivy-clad ruin, Castle Hackett dates back to the thirteenth century, when it was built by the Hackett family, Normans who settled on the east side of Lough Corrib, having driven the O'Flahertys across the lake to Connemara. The castle lies at the foot of Knockma Hill, best known as the home of Finvarra, king of the Connacht fairies, while Queen Maeve of Connacht is reputed to have been buried there.

The Hacketts remained here for at least two centuries, until the castle was taken by the Kirwans, one of the Tribes of Galway, who settled there in the fifteenth century. The Kirwans built a new three-storey house called Castlehacket in the early eighteenth century and added to it substantially a century later, but the house was badly burned in 1923 and rebuilt some years later, and this still stands today.

Castle Matrix

RATHKEALE, COUNTY LIMERICK

Off the beaten track and difficult to find, Castle Matrix is a fifteenth-century fortress, built for the Earls of Desmond and later granted to the Southwell family, who converted it into a manor house. Sir Thomas Southwell, who was a key figure in bringing German Protestant refugees to Ireland, settled one hundred families on his estate in 1709.

The English explorer Sir Walter Raleigh stayed at Castle Matrix in 1580, and invited the poet Edmund Spenser to visit (1552–99). It's said that Raleigh presented some Virginia tubers to his host Edmund Southwell, who planted these potatoes in the land around the castle and later distributed them throughout Munster. By the 1960s, the castle had fallen into disrepair, when it was bought by Colonel Sean O'Driscoll, an American architect, who restored it. It is now privately owned by his widow.

Castle Pook

CASTLEPOOK SOUTH, NEAR DONERAILE, COUNTY CORK

Dating back to the 1380s, Castle Pook is a five-storey Norman tower house, standing on a rocky outcrop against the backdrop of the Ballyhoura Mountains. The castle was built by Geoffrey the Red, of the Norman Synan family, who arrived in Ireland with Strongbow. The family seemed to have run into financial difficulties in the sixteenth century, but received a pardon of its debts to the Crown in 1573, and a similar pardon in 1601. The Synans seem to have occupied Castle Pook, or Fowke, as it was then known, for four hundred years but, by the eighteenth century, the castle had passed to the Morgan family, whose notable members include Richard Morgan, who died at Castle Pook, aged 107, in 1748. He had been clerk of the Court of Peace for the county in the time of James II. Privately owned, the castle is to be renovated by its Swiss-based owner.

Castlegarde Castle

CAPPAMORE, COUNTY LIMERICK
+353 61 381 435 | *www.castlegardecastle.ie*

Said to be among the oldest inhabited castles in Ireland, Castlegarde was built by Donal Mór O'Brien and his sister-in-law Aoife McMurrough (Strongbow's wife) around 1190. The castle has had many owners down the centuries, including the Earl of Bath. The structure includes a murder hole, moat, and bawn, with an 1820 Georgian addition, which was designed by the notable Pain Brothers architects. Over the main entrance is a stone sculpture of the head of Brian Boru, High King of Munster and then of Ireland, who was killed after his victory at the Battle of Clontarf against the Danes in 1014.

The current owners, David and Hazel Thompson, have carried out extensive restoration work over many years, which they fund with private tours of the castle, accompanied by tea and scones.

Castletown House

CASTLETOWN, CELBRIDGE, COUNTY KILDARE, W23 V9H3
+353 1 6288252 | www.castletown.ie

Castletown House is Ireland's first and foremost Palladian-style mansion, built in the 1720s for the then speaker of the Irish House of Commons, William Conolly. It was built as a central block with two connected wings on either side, housing the kitchens and stables, with much Italian architectural influence but overseen by the Irish architect Edward Pearce.

Conolly was the son of an innkeeper in Donegal, who trained as a lawyer in Dublin and made a fortune dealing with the confiscation of lands after the war between James II of England and William of Orange, and at the same time marrying well. His ability and good fortune meant that, when he died in 1729, he was the wealthiest politician in Ireland.

The house was improved by the wife of one of his heirs, Lady Louisa Conolly, who, like William Conolly, had no children. She devoted herself to decoration and entertainment at Castletown House and added many of its finest features, such as the Staircase Hall, Dining Room, Print Room, and Long Gallery.

The house, along with 120 acres, is now in the ownership of the State. The parklands are open daily and the house is open for most of the year for tours.

Classiebawn Castle

There are few more dramatic views on the Wild Atlantic Way in County Sligo than Classiebawn Castle, set against the backdrop of Bunbulben mountain with the sea crashing below. Classiebawn is a private property and so can only be appreciated from a distance. Built towards the end of his life by the statesman Lord Palmerston, the Victorian castle became the summer home of Lord Louis Mountbatten, a member of the British royal family, who was assassinated aboard his boat along with three others as it set out from nearby Mullaghmore harbour in 1979. Prince Charles and his wife Camilla made an emotional visit to the area in 2015 to honour the memory of his beloved great-uncle.

Clogh Oughter Castle

COUNTY CAVAN

Standing proud on a tiny island in the middle of a lake in County Cavan, about four kilometres from the village Killeshandra, Clogh Oughter Castle is falling gently into ruin, but cannonballs, rather than nature, dealt the first blow. The castle is said to have been built around 1220 and fortified in the 1230s. During the Plantation of Ulster in 1610, Clogh Oughter Castle became a prison. It's most famous as the death place of Owen Roe O'Neill, in 1649. By late 1652, Cromwellian forces had overrun Ireland. Clogh Oughter was the final fortified outpost. There was a siege, followed by the surrender, and Cromwell's army demolished most of the south side of the castle, leaving the ruin that stands today.

A visit to the castle can be arranged by contacting Cavan Canoe Centre, where guided boat trips can be organized.

Clontarf Castle

CASTLE AVENUE, CLONTARF EAST, DUBLIN, D03 N974
+353 1 833 2321 | *www.clontarfcastle.ie*

Clontarf Castle is an 1830s Tudor Revival castle incorporating an older tower, on the site of a medieval castle said to date from 1172. Clontarf was held by the Knights Templar and, after their suppression in 1308, passed to the Knights Hospitaller, until confiscated during the Dissolution of the Monasteries. In 1600 Queen Elizabeth I of England granted the estate to Sir Geoffrey Fenton, and it passed by marriage from his descendants to the King family. After Cromwell's conquest of Ireland, the Clontarf estate was given to Captain John Blackwell, who later sold it John Vernon, a general in Cromwell's army. The Vernon family was to remain in possession for some three hundred years. The last of the Vernons to own Clontarf Castle was Edward Kingston Vernon (1869–1967). The castle was finally sold out of the family and became a hotel, which it remains today.

Crom Castle

NEWTOWN BUTLER, COUNTY FERMANAGH, BT92 8AP
+44 28 677 38004 | *www.cromcastle.com*

Seat of the Crichton family, Earls of Erne, Crom Castle
sits on around 1900 acres on the shores of Lough Erne.
The estate is managed by the National Trust, and is open
to the public. While the estate dates back some eight
hundred years, the castle itself was built in 1820, designed
by the same architect responsible for Buckingham Palace,
Edward Blore. The 3rd Earl is remembered as the
employer of Captain Charles Boycott, whose manhandling
of relations with agricultural workers on Lord Erne's estate
in County Mayo caused a political and public outcry
and gave the English language the term "to boycott".
The west wing, owned by the current Viscount Crichton,
can be hired for weddings and other events.

Dangan Castle

TRIM, COUNTY MEATH

The eighteenth-century seat of the Wellesley family, and the childhood home of Britain's greatest general, Arthur Wellesley (1769–1852), the first Duke of Wellington, Dangan Castle is now a ruin. Beside it are the remains of a medieval tower house, which had been the original home of the Wellesleys, who settled in Meath in the fifteenth century.

The later house was built by Richard Wesley (c. 1690–1758), first Baron of Mornington. He spent lavishly on the grounds and it's said that at one time the estate boasted over one hundred follies and garden buildings, of which just one obelisk survives today. As the third son of the house, Arthur Wellesley's prospects were poor but he made his name in the army, rising to become a military hero after his victory over Napoleon at Waterloo, and twice serving as Prime Minister.

Desmond Castle

CORK STREET, SLEVEEN, KINSALE, COUNTY CORK
+353 21 477 4855 | www.heritageireland.ie

Built by the Earl of Desmond around 1500, Desmond Castle has served many purposes down the centuries, including those of customs house, prison, and army stores. In 1600 and 1601, it was used as an arsenal by Don Juan Aguilla during the Spanish occupation of the town, which lasted for one hundred days, prior to the Battle of Kinsale in 1601.

Kinsale was a designated Wine Port, and supplied ships from 1412 for the Vintage Fleet. Today Desmond Castle houses the International Museum of Wine, an exhibition that tells the story of Ireland's Wine Geese – the Irish families who went to France, Spain, Australia, and California, and found work in the wine trade.

The roots of the Wine Geese lie in the flight of the "Wild Geese", the soldiers who fled from Ireland to France after the Treaty of Limerick in 1691. Sometimes they travelled on the French ships that smuggled wine into the west coast of Ireland, described on the ships' manifests as "wild geese", evoking the lonely calls of birds travelling winter skies.

Doe Castle

CREESLOUGH, COUNTY DONEGAL | *www.heritageireland.ie*

Doe Castle is strategically located on an inlet of Sheephaven Bay and surrounded by water on three sides. Dating from the mid fifteenth century, it was a stronghold of the MacSweeney clan, who came to Donegal from Scotland as Gallowglasses, or mercenary soldiers.

It is said that survivors from the Spanish Armada were sheltered here by the MacSweeneys.

Abandoned around 1700, the castle fell into ruin, before being restored as a residence in 1810 by the Donegal MP George Vaughan Hart, who made his home there until 1864. His initials can be seen above the doorway on the east side of the keep.

Doe Castle was renovated by the Office of Public Works (OPW) in the 1990s. The castle grounds are open daily and tours are available during the summer months.

Donegal Castle

SAINT HELENES, 11 CASTLE STREET, MILLTOWN, DONEGAL, F94 E3W5

+353 74 972 2405

Donegal is O'Donnell country. The O'Donnell clan can trace its lineage back to the fifth century, and Donegal Castle was one of its many strongholds. The earliest parts of the castle, built on a bend of the Eske river, date back to the fourteenth century. In 1611, during the Plantation of Ulster, the castle and its lands were granted to an English army man, Captain Basil Brooke. The tower was damaged by the departing O'Donnells to prevent the castle being used against the Gaelic clans, but was quickly restored by its new owner. Brooke also added windows, a gable, and a large manor house, complete with turrets.

The castle fell into disrepair in the eighteenth century, and it was not until the 1990s that it was fully restored and opened to the public. Notable features include a trip stairwell (uneven stairs designed to trip up enemies) and a garderobe, or inner toilet chamber with the chute angled in such a way that enemy archers could not attack in an unguarded moment.

The castle is furnished throughout and decorated with Persian rugs and French tapestries.

Drimnagh Castle

LONGMILE ROAD, DUBLIN 12

+353 1 450 2530 | *www.drimnaghcastle.org*

Drimnagh Castle is something of a rarity, being the only Irish castle that is still surrounded by a flooded moat. The castle dates from the 1240s, when it was built by a Norman knight, Hugo de Berneval, who was part of Strongbow's first invasion of Ireland and thus granted a large estate for his services to the English king. He built Drimnagh on high ground as a defence against the local clans and those who made regular forays from the Wicklow hills. Their name anglicized to Barnwell, the family stayed at Drimnagh for the next four hundred years, acquiring lands all the way to Balbriggan on the north Dublin coast. The castle, built of local grey limestone, consists of a restored Great Hall and medieval undercroft, a tall battlement tower with lookout posts, and other separate buildings, including stables, old coach house, dairy, and folly tower.

Drishane Castle

MILLSTREET, COUNTY CORK

Divorce was not legalized in Ireland until 1996 but, ninety years earlier, an Act of Parliament allowed for the sensational divorce between Henry Aubrey Beaumont Wallis of Drishane Castle in County Cork and his estranged wife Elizabeth Bingham. The Wallis family had owned Drishane since around 1709, after it was previously owned by the MacCarthy clan and the Hollow Sword Blade Company, which sold it to one Henry Wallis. For the next two hundred years the Wallis family lived occasionally at Drishane, enhancing the castle in the Victorian era with baronial flourishes such as battlements and corner towers. The property was eventually sold to a French religious order, which ran it as a boarding school for girls until the early 1990s. It was then bought by a local family, and is now a centre for asylum seekers.

Dromoland Castle

DROMOLAND, NEWMARKET ON FERGUS, COUNTY CLARE, V95 ATD3

+353 61 368 144 | *www.dromoland.ie*

The hereditary seat of the O'Brien clan, descended from the O'Brien High Kings of Ireland, Dromoland Castle is now a luxury five-star hotel.

It's one of at least three castles to have been built on the estate, near the village of Newmarket-on-Fergus. The present castle, with its castellated turrets, was built in 1835 in a romantic baronial style that also manages to feel homely. A Gothic porch to the north front displays the O'Brien arms. Inside a series of comfortable public rooms lead off a wide vaulted hallway, which is repeated on the upper floor, where bedrooms are accessed from a landing with exquisite Gothic ceiling decorations.

The O'Brien family sold Dromoland in 1962.

Dromore Castle

Rising from the shore of the Shannon Estuary, Dromore Castle looks like a fairytale medieval castle, but in fact it was built in the mid nineteenth century for the third Earl of Limerick to a design by the somewhat eccentric architect E. W. Goodwin. Goodwin, who was a friend of Oscar Wilde, researched medieval Irish buildings and included a round tower to evoke the silhouette of the Rock of Cashel. Its highly unusual features incorporate elements of old Irish architecture, such as a round tower, Celtic crosses, a Norman keep, and a church. Goodwin also designed the furniture and many stained glass windows for the castle but these have all since disappeared and the castle is now falling into ruin.

Dublin Castle

DAME STREET, DUBLIN 2
+353 1 645 8800 | *www.dublincastle.ie*

One of the most important castles in Ireland, Dublin Castle was the seat of English and British rule in Ireland from 1204 until 1922. Built on elevated ground on the site of an Viking settlement, it was originally a medieval fortress in rectangular shape with bastions at each corner, beside which the river Poddle flowed into a dark pool, or *Dubh Linn*, which gave Dublin its name. The castle could then be reached by boat from the river Liffey, which was wider in those days.

An extensive fire in 1684 caused much damage to what was still the original fortress and, after this, work was undertaken to transform it into a Georgian palace with State Apartments, where the Viceroy lived and entertained, occasionally joined by the British monarch. The early nineteenth century saw the addition of the Chapel Royal, a gothic revival structure that is a highlight of the castle now. Despite these splendid Georgian additions, visitors can still see parts of the original medieval and Viking structures today.

Dublin Castle has been at the centre of historical events in Ireland from its inception until it was handed over to the Irish State Government, in 1922. It is now open to visitors, who can enjoy the castle, as well as libraries and museums.

Dunamase Castle

AGHNAHILY, COUNTY LAOIS

+353 57 866 4129

Few castles in Ireland possess as impressive a setting as that of Dunamase, a medieval stone fortress built atop a limestone outcrop in County Laois, also known as the Rock of Dunamase. The site once hosted an ancient Irish native fort, dating from at least the early Christian period, and Dunamase is believed to have been plundered by the Vikings about 845.

Centuries later, a motte-and-bailey castle was built on the earlier fortress and, in turn, was rebuilt and enlarged in about 1250.

Partially destroyed by Cromwell's men in 1650, the castle was renovated again in the eighteenth century but later abandoned, and is now in ruins.

Dunboy Castle and Puxley Manor

DUNBOY, NEAR CASTLETOWNBERE, COUNTY CORK

Built to defend the harbour of Berehaven, Dunboy Castle is said to have been the seat of clan leader O'Sullivan Bere, who collected taxes from fishing vessels sheltering in the harbour. Such was his power that Elizabeth I sent a substantial army to overthrow him. A bloody battle ensued at Dunboy Castle and all inhabitants perished or were executed. The castle was left in ruins and was never restored.

Near the ruins is a second, much later, castle called Puxley Manor, an extravagant Gothic pile built in the late 1800s for Henry Lavallin Puxley, owner of the Berehaven Copper Mines.

The Puxley mansion was burned by the IRA in June 1921. In the early 2000s, the castle was renovated with the intention of converting it into a luxury hotel, but the project was never completed.

Dungarvan Castle

CASTLE STREET, DUNGARVAN, COUNTY WATERFORD,
X35 DV58 | +353 58 48144

Dungarvan Castle was built in 1185 by the Anglo-Normans
at a strategic location at the entrance to Dungarvan
Harbour. The mighty fortress later served as a barracks for
British soldiers. In 1922, it was taken by the IRA and burned
to the ground. After restoration, the castle nowadays
opens its doors to visitors from May to September.

Dungiven Castle

DUNGIVEN, LONDONDERRY, BT47 4LQ

Dungiven Castle was the ancestral home of the O'Cahans, who ruled this area for hundreds of years. In 1607, Sir Donnell O'Cahan had his lands and titles confiscated. He escaped to mainland Europe at the time of the Flight of the Earls. This episode is reputed to have inspired the song "Danny Boy", which was originally called "O'Cahan's Lament".

The present-day castle largely dates from 1836 and was built by Robert Ogilby, who died before its completion. It was used for housing the US Army during the Second World War, and later was used as a dance hall during the 1950s and 1960s, playing host to Tom Jones and Engelbert Humperdinck, among others.

Dunguaire Castle

DUNGORY EAST, KINVARRA, COUNTY GALWAY

+353 61 711 200 | *www.dunguairecastle.com*

Said to be one of the most photographed castles in Ireland, Dunguaire Castle is perched overlooking Galway Bay, just outside the seaside village of Kinvara. Dunguaire dates from around 1520, but it takes its name from the nearby ancient fort of Guaire Aidne mac Colmáin, the legendary king of Connacht and head of the Hynes clan since the seventh century.

In the early seventeenth century, the castle passed into the hands of the Martyns of Galway, whose family owned it until the twentieth century. In 1924, Dunguaire was bought and renovated by Oliver St John Gogarty, a literary figure and surgeon, who established it as a meeting place for Celtic revival poets and playwrights, such as W. B. Yeats and George Bernard Shaw. Renovations were completed by Lady Christabel Ampthill, who bought Dunguaire after the Second World War. The interior of the four-storey tower house is currently open to the public as a tourist attraction and medieval-style banquets are held there through the summer months.

Dunluce Castle

BUSHMILLS, COUNTY ANTRIM, BT57 8UY
+44 28 2073 1938 | *dunluce.castle@communities-ni.gov.uk*

Perched atop sheer cliffs and approached by a bridge, the spectacular ruins of Dunluce Castle are among Northern Ireland's most popular tourist attractions. Built by the McQuillan family around 1500, the castle has a long and bloody history of invasion, war, and rebellion. It was seized by the MacDonnell clan in the 1550s, under the leadership of the chieftain Sorley Boy MacDonnell. In the seventeenth century, Dunluce was the seat of the earls of County Antrim, and saw the establishment of a small town in 1608. Visitors can explore the findings of archaeological digs within the cobbled streets and stone merchants' houses of the long-abandoned Dunluce town. The dramatic setting has inspired artists for centuries – Dunluce is said to have been the inspiration for the royal castle of Cair Paravel in C. S. Lewis's Narnia stories, and more recently it has featured as the stronghold of Pyke on the Iron Islands in *Game of Thrones*.

Dunsany Castle

DUNSANY, COUNTY MEATH

+353 46 902 5169 | *www.dunsany.com*

Dunsany Castle is a Norman castle, started around 1181 by Hugh de Lacy, who also commissioned neighbouring Killeen Castle, as well as Trim Castle. Dunsany is said to be Ireland's oldest home in continuous occupation, having been held by the Cusack family and their descendants by marriage, the Plunketts, to the present day. The castle is surrounded by a large estate that includes its own church, a walled garden, a house, and numerous outbuildings. Open to the public on certain days of the year, the castle has richly decorated and furnished public rooms that were extended and embellished in the 18th and 19th centuries in the Gothic baronial and Arts and Crafts style.

Dunsany Castle had an important role to play in Irish fashion: it was here in July 1953 that Carmel Snow, the Irish-born editor of *Harper's Bazaar*, brought a group of American fashion buyers and journalists, along with the photographer Richard Avedon. They were introduced to Irish couturier Sybil Connolly, who went on to become one of Jacqueline Kennedy's favourite designers.

Dysert O'Dea Castle

DYSERT, COROFIN, COUNTY CLARE
+353 65 683 7401 | www.dysertcastle.com

Built over a twenty-year period from around 1470, the now restored Dysert O'Dea Castle is home to the Clare Archaeological Society and houses a fine collection of artefacts from the Stone Age to the twentieth century.

The castle has many typical features of a medieval tower house, such as narrow loophole windows and a murder hole. The five-storey-high tower house was built in 1480 by Diarmaid O'Dea, Lord of Cineal Fearmaic, and was the home of the O'Dea chiefs until 1692. The upper floors were badly damaged by Cromwellian forces in 1651.

Starting from the castle, there is a four-kilometre archaeological trail, with up to twenty-five original monuments, including a richly decorated twelfth-century high cross dedicated to St Tola, a holy well, a round tower, Iron Age stone forts, Bronze Age cooking places, and a Romanesque church.

Glenveagh Castle

GLENVEAGH NATIONAL PARK, GARTAN MOUNTAIN,
CHURCH HILL, COUNTY DONEGAL
+353 76 100 2537 | www.glenveaghnationalpark.ie

Glenveagh Castle was built around 1870, as a castellated mansion, by a wealthy Irish land speculator called Captain John Adair, who had made his fortune in the USA. He returned with his wife Cornelia, the daughter of a general on the victorious Union side in the American Civil War, and bought a large estate in Donegal, where they built this castle in baronial style with a rectangular four-storey keep. He purchased some 28,000 acres of land with the aim of creating a highland retreat to rival any other, in the process cruelly evicting hundreds of tenants from the land just to improve its appearance. After his death, his wife remained in part residence for many years and treated the tenants more fairly.

The castle's American connection continued with the purchase of the castle in 1938 by an art connoisseur called Henry Plumer McIlhenny from Philadelphia, who eventually left the castle and gardens to the Irish State in 1979. It now forms the Glenveagh National Park, at the centre of which are the castle and its courtyards, walled garden, pleasure grounds, and woodland gardens, open for visits and tours.

Glin Castle

GLIN DEMESNE, COUNTY LIMERICK, V94 VF68
+353 87 329 4575 | *enquiries@glin-castle.com*

Ancestral seat of the Knights of Glin for over seven
hundred years, Glin Castle overlooks the river Shannon,
thirty-two miles from Limerick. The Gothic façade of the
castle gives the building a fairytale quality, which continues
inside with a quintessential country house atmosphere.
The castle was built for entertaining, with a magnificent
hallway featuring Corinthian columns and an ornate
Adams-style ceiling overhead. It was faithfully maintained
by its late owner Desmond Fitzgerald, an authority on
Irish furniture, and his wife Olda, who together furnished
it with museum-quality Irish furniture. Its richly decorated
rooms are regularly rented out for weddings and events,
and the castle also offers accommodation and garden visits.

Gosford Castle

MARKETHILL, COUNTY ARMAGH, BT60 1GD

The castle, used as Riverrun in the third series of *Game of Thrones*, was once in such a poor state of repair that the owners offered to sell it for just £1 to anyone who would commit to refurbishing the crumbling structure. The castle dates from the mid nineteenth century, when it and much of the surrounding village were built by the second Earl of Gosford, Archibald Acheson. Gosford was home to the family until 1921 and, during the Second World War, it was used as a base for Allied troops and as a prisoner-of-war camp. Postwar, the Acheson family sold the castle to the Ministry for Agriculture, which developed a conservation forest in the 590-acre grounds. During the Troubles, the castle was used as a military base and, later still, it operated as a hotel, before being abandoned. By 2002, the castle had fallen into serious disrepair but was later developed as luxury apartments.

Hatch's Castle

48 MARKET STREET, ARDEE, COUNTY LOUTH
+353 87 276 9138 | *www.booking.com*

One of two castles that punctuate the main street of the market town of Ardee in County Louth, Hatch's Castle might scandalize purists with its later additions of large sash windows and a Georgian front door, but the result is a cosy castle that has been in continuous occupation since it was built some time around 1600.

The castle takes its name from Thomas Hatch, a merchant who acquired it in the 1750s and whose family lived there for two centuries. The four-storey tower, crowned with a wall walk and battlements, was substantially remodelled in the nineteenth century but plenty of its original features remain. It's now run as a B & B.

Helen's Tower

CLANDEBOYE ROAD, BANGOR, BT23 4RX
+44 28 9127 0371 | *www.irishlandmark.com*

Helen's Tower is a nineteenth-century folly built on the estate of Frederick Temple Blackwood, the Baron of Clandeboye, on the highest point of his estate, with distant views of Scotland, the Isle of Man, and Wales. The Baron commissioned architect William Burn to design the tower in the Scottish baronial style and then named it for his mother, Helen. A poem in honour of Helen, composed, by Tennyson, is engraved on a brass plate in the tower.

During the First World War, soldiers of the 36th Ulster Division trained on the Clandeboye estate before being sent to fight on the Somme. A replica of Helen's Tower, the Ulster Tower, was built at Thiepval, in the Somme Department, in 1921, as a memorial to the men of the 36th who were killed in battle.

Hillsborough Castle & Gardens

THE SQUARE, HILLSBOROUGH, BT26 6AG
+44 28 9268 1308

Hillsborough Castle is a working royal palace, functioning as the official residence of the British Royal Family when they are in Northern Ireland, and it has been the home of the Secretary of State since the 1970s. It was built for the Hill family, who rose to prominence in the eighteenth century, acquiring titles and lands and various businesses, including linen mills. In 1922, the family sold Hillsborough to the British government, which needed a new base from which to govern the six counties of Northern Ireland. The Queen first came here as a princess in 1945. Following a four-year refurbishment, visitors now enjoy its elegant State Rooms and Throne Room, which are furnished with valuable antiques and Royal Family mementos and photographs.

Hope Castle

CASTLEBLAYNEY, COUNTY MONAGHAN

Also known as Blayney Castle, this once splendid Georgian mansion was built near the site of an earlier Plantation castle that gave the surrounding town its name. The castle is now boarded up, having suffered a fire in 2010. Approached via an impressive gateway from the town that leads into public parkland, Castle Hope has had a number of occupants since it was sold in 1853 by the twelfth and last Lord Blayney. The buyer then was Henry Thomas Hope, part of whose inheritance from his uncle, Henry Phillip Hope, was the famous Hope Diamond, which was sold by the family in 1901 to pay off debts. Henry renovated the castle and embellished its façade with scrolled cresting on the roof parapets and a canopy of ornamental cast iron and glass.

It is now owned by the local county council and remains closed.

Howth Castle

COUNTY DUBLIN

+353 1 832 1027 | *www.howthcastle.com*

This massive medieval keep has been the home of the
St Lawrences for eight hundred years, since 1177, when
Almeric, the first Lord of Howth, came to Ireland.
Legend has it that the pirate queen Granuaile, or
Grace O'Malley, as she was also known, once came to
the house in 1576 hoping to dine with Lord Howth,
and found the gates locked against her. Furious at this
breach of hospitality, she kidnapped Lord Howth's infant
heir, who was on the beach nearby. She returned him on
the condition that the house remain open at mealtimes
and that an extra place always be laid for her descendants.
The house contains original furniture, paintings, and
artefacts, including a portrait by Jonathan Swift and the
Great Sword of Howth. Private tours can be arranged
through the website. However, the castle and grounds
were recently bought by Tetrarch Capital, who plan on
turning the estate into a major tourist destination.

Huntington Castle

CLONEGAL, COUNTY CARLOW

+353 53 937 7160 | *www.huntingtoncastle.com*

The original tower house of Huntington Castle was built by Laurence, the first (and last) Lord Esmonde, in 1625 and was used as a garrison under Cromwell because of its strategic location in the Slaney Valley, between the counties of Wexford and Carlow.

Located in the sleepy village of Clonegal, it is set among manicured gardens that include a spectacular yew walk and is owned by the Durdin-Robertsons. Several apparitions are claimed to have been seen by guests and family members alike in the old hallways and historic rooms.

The castle and grounds are open to visitors by arrangement, and rooms are also available to rent on Airbnb.

Inchiquin Castle

COUNTY CLARE

It's said that the pedigree of the O'Brien clan, the Lords Inchiquin, is kept in a vault at Lloyds in London and is thirty-six feet (nearly eleven metres) in length, but the grand dynasty that once ruled County Clare may have had its roots in this modest castle, which now lies in ruins. Little remains here except the remnants of a barbican tower, standing on a rocky peninsula jutting into the north side of Lake Inchiquin.

It is not known who exactly erected the structure or when. It may have been the Lord of Thomond, Teige O'Brien, who died in 1466, as he is the first recorded resident and the architectural features coincide with his era.

The castle was abandoned towards the end of the seventeenth century and has not been occupied since.

Isert Kelly Castle

CASTLEPARK, KILCHREEST, COUNTY GALWAY

A tower house built in the fifteenth century, Isert Kelly was the seat of the MacHubert Burkes, a family that claimed its lineage back to Hubert, son of Richard Óg de Burgh, who was a Hiberno-Norman knight in the thirteenth century.

After Cromwell's invasion, the castle passed into the hands of Dudley Persse, and the Persse family seemed to have owned it until well into the nineteenth century.

Isert Kelly Castle was excavated in 2014 and is still undergoing some work, mostly on the collapsed bawn, which is hidden under a grassy bank. The well-preserved tower stands twenty-one metres tall and is surrounded by the remains of a sixty-metre-square bawn. The main room is situated on the third storey. It has a fireplace dated at 1604 with the initials W. H.

Jigginstown Castle

NEWBRIDGE ROAD, NAAS, COUNTY KILDARE
www.kildare.ie

A castle planned for a king's visit but never completed, Jigginstown, near Naas in County Kildare, was the grand design of Thomas Wentworth, first Earl of Strafford and Lord Deputy of Ireland. He hoped to entertain Charles I of England, and set about building the castle around 1637, spending an estimated £6000. Not only did the king not come to visit, but Wentworth was summoned to London, accused of treason, and imprisoned in the Tower of London. The king, to whom Wentworth had been loyal, signed an act of Parliament which resulted in his execution in 1641.

Jigginstown was never finished and, by the 1650s, the house was in ruins and most of the lead and iron used in its construction had been removed for use as ammunition.

Johnstown Castle

COUNTY WEXFORD

+353 53 918 4671 | *www.johnstowncastle.ie*

Johnstown is a restored nineteenth-century Gothic Revival castle with stunning ornamental gardens.

It's a popular spot for walks and picnics, with a huge variety of exotic trees and shrubs. The estate was once the home of two prominent Wexford families, the first of which were the Esmondes, a Norman family that settled in Wexford in the twelfth century. The estate was confiscated after the invasion of Cromwell and came into the hands of John Grogan in 1692. Grogan's family remained there until 1945, when they gave the estate to the Irish State.

Johnstown estate was continually developed from its humble beginnings as a tower house, to a turreted and castellated castle in 1863, with the grounds extending to one thousand acres. The castle and grounds, including an agricultural museum and intriguing servants' tunnel, is now owned by Teagasc, an agricultural research body, and can be toured. The ornamental grounds and garden were designed by Daniel Robertson, who also designed Powerscourt Gardens in Wicklow. There are many winding pathways for visitors to venture around the gardens and the two lakes, with scenic folly towers, inhabited by a range of geese, swans, and ducks.

Jordan's Castle

ARDGLASS, COUNTY DOWN

Ardglass, once an important port town in the Anglo-Norman Earldom of Ulster, has no less than four medieval tower houses, of which Jordan's Castle is the most notable.

There is very little architectural evidence to help pin a definitive date on the castle. Window details suggest fifteenth century but they have been reconstructed too much to tell.

The earliest historical record of the castle is when it was defended by Simon Jordan against the O'Neill clan for a period of three years, until its relief by Lord Mountjoy in 1601. At one stage, a stone carved with the arms of the Jordan family is said to have been embedded in the castle walls but this stone can no longer be found.

In 1911, the castle was bought by Francis Joseph Bigger, an antiquarian from Belfast who carried out renovations and opened it to the public under the name Castleshane. He used it to show and store a collection of antiques. After his death in 1926, it was given to the State, under the condition that it be preserved as an ancient monument.

Kanturk Castle

BANTEER, COUNTY CORK
www.antaisce.org/properties/kanturk-castle

Legend has it that Kanturk Castle was built by seven stonemasons all named John, and work commenced around 1601 and continued for several years. The four-storey castle, with five-storey towers at each of its four corners, was built for MacDonagh MacCarthy, Lord of Dunhallow and a member of the powerful MacCarthy clan, which dominated much of the southwest of Ireland. However, work on the castle was stopped in 1618, possibly after English settlers in the area objected to the castle being too large and too fortified, or it's also possible that MacCarthy simply ran out of money to finish it. It was an elaborate structure for its time, showcasing the new Tudor architecture, with Renaissance doorways and mullioned windows and several fireplaces, all of which are visible today.

Dermot MacCarthy, into whose hands the castle later came, mortgaged it in 1641 to Sir Philip Perceval, who took out many of the fixtures.

Kanturk Castle was passed down through various families until 1900, when it was donated to the National Trust Committee for Ireland on the unusual condition that it be kept in the same condition as it was when handed over, i.e. a ruin.

Kilcash Castle

CLONMEL, COUNTY TIPPERARY
www.tipperary.com/kilcash-castle

Kilcash Castle was built around 1540 for the Butlers, Earls of Ormonde, who ruled the county of Tipperary and had a number of other bases, including Carrick-on-Suir and Roscrea Castles. Kilcash passed through several lines of the Butler family, and eventually to John Butler, the seventeenth Earl of Ormonde. The last recorded event at the castle was his funeral in 1795, when he was buried, like most of the Butlers, in the graveyard adjoining the castle. Five years later the castle was largely demolished. What survives is an ivy-clad tower house and the partial remains of the great hall. The castle is immortalized in a poem, "Lament for Kilcash" ("Caoineadh Cill Chais"), which begins: "Cad a dheanfhaimid feasta gan adhmad" ("What will we do for timber") and which mourns the passing of Margaret Burke, the castle's most celebrated lady. She was a daughter of the Earl of Clanrickard, and the widow of Brian McGuinness, Viscount Iveagh, from County Down. She was then married to Thomas Butler, and during their lifetime, in the late seventeenth and early eighteenth centuries, Kilcash was known for its great hospitality and as a refuge for Catholics.

Kilclief Castle

SHORE ROAD, STRANGFORD, COUNTY DOWN
+44 28 9082 3207 | *www.communities-ni.gov.uk/topics/*
historic-environment

John Sely, the Bishop of Down, was threatened with excommunication in 1434 if he did not cast off his mistress, a married woman by the name of Lettice Thomas. Scandalously for the time, Sely had been publicly living in his summer residence, Kilclief Castle in County Down, with Thomas and, despite the threat of excommunication, they continued to live together for several more years. In 1441 the archbishop finally managed to remove Sely from his position, and history loses track of the couple after that. Kilclief Castle dates from around 1413 and it's said to have been the earliest tower house in County Down. Some of its features, including a machicolation arch, projecting towers, and spiral staircases, may have been copied in the building of later towers at Ardglass, Strangford, and various other sites.

Kilcolman Castle

NEAR BUTTEVANT, COUNTY CORK

Kilcolman Castle lies in ruins today but in the 1420s the four-storey fortified tower was home to James FitzGerald, sixth Earl of Desmond, whose clan controlled vast tracts of Munster. The Desmonds' lands and Kilcolman were later confiscated by the English Crown after the Second Desmond Rebellion (1579–83), and the castle and over three thousand acres were granted to the poet Edmund Spenser (1552–99). Spenser settled in Kilcolman from the late 1580s, refurbishing the castle and making a home at Kilcolman with his second wife, Elizabeth Boyle.

In 1598, during the Nine Years' War, Kilcolman Castle was destroyed by the forces of Hugh O'Neill, Earl of Tyrone. Spenser escaped and his son Sylvanus rebuilt Kilcolman, but it was again destroyed in 1622, and afterwards abandoned.

Kilkenny Castle

+353 56 770 4100 | *www.kilkenycastle.ie*

The ancestral seat of the Ormonde Butlers dominates the medieval town of Kilkenny with its turreted round towers and magnificent ornate gateway. It was built in 1190 by Strongbow's son-in-law, William Marshall, Earl of Pembroke. His heirs sold it to the third Earl of Ormonde around 1391. The castle has been much extended and enlarged over the centuries, including an extensive remodelling in Victorian times. Each year, hundreds of thousands of visitors come to see this grand country house and walk through its acres of parkland; and explore a formal terraced rose garden, woodlands, and a man-made lake, which were added in the nineteenth century. There is also a tearoom, a playground, and several orienteering trails. The castle was handed over to the people of Kilkenny by Arthur Butler, Earl of Ormonde in 1967, and was extensively restored in the 1970s.

Killeen Castle

DUNSANY, COUNTY MEATH

+353 689 3000 | *www.killeencastle.com*

Ancestral home of the Plunkett Family, Earls of Fingall, Killeen Castle dates from the twelfth century, when it and a nearby castle, Dunsany, were founded by Hugh de Lacy in 1181. Both castles passed by marriage around 1403 into the Plunkett family, many of whom are buried in a small church in the grounds of Killeen, and descendants of whom still reside in Dunsany Castle.

Killeen Castle was greatly enlarged in 1804 for the eighth Earl, and was later remodelled in the style of Windsor Castle, with the addition of battlements and turrets.

The castle was sold in 1978, and suffered an arson attack by the IRA in 1981 during the Hunger Strike. It was later sold to a property developer, who has preserved it with a long-term plan to fully restore the interior and convert it to a hotel.

Killua Castle

CLONMELLON, COUNTY WESTMEATH, C15 EWF2
+353 87 943 6727 | *www.killuacastle.com*

A Gothic Revival castle with links to Sir Walter Raleigh and Lawrence of Arabia, Killua Castle was rescued from complete ruin in recent years and has been carefully restored. The land surrounding the castle was originally owned by the Knights Hospitallers of St John but were confiscated by Cromwell, who granted the estate to one of his captains, Benjamin Chapman, around 1667. The original house dates from 1780 but a major refurbishment fifty years later transformed it into a castle with battlements, a round tower, and the addition of a castellated wing. It sits in a large demesne, with lakes and follies and an obelisk commemorating the alleged planting of the first potato in Ireland by Sir Walter Raleigh, a cousin of the Chapmans.

Killua Castle is open to the public at weekends and by appointment.

Killymoon Castle

KILLYMOON ROAD, COOKSTOWN, COUNTY TYRONE

+44 28 867 69949 | *www.discovernorthernireland.com/killymoon-castle*

Nestled in woodlands high above the Ballinderry River, Killymoon is one of a small number of Irish castles designed by the celebrated English architect, John Nash, whose work includes the remodelling of Buckingham Palace, Marble Arch, and the Royal Pavilion in Brighton, as well as numerous London houses.

Killymoon Castle was built around 1803 for Colonel James Stewart MP, whose family had owned the surrounding estate since the 1640s. Built at a reputed cost of £80,000 (over £7.5 million today), the walled demesne was written about in the *Irish Penny Journal* of 1841. In 1850 the property was sold, following the decease of the colonel's son, William Stewart, who was a bachelor.

Kilwaughter Castle

THE DEMESNE, KILWAUGHTER, LARNE, COUNTY ANTRIM,
BT40 2PE | *www.kilwaughtercastle.com*

Kilwaughter was designed by the celebrated architect John Nash for the Agnew family who came to Antrim from Scotland during the Ulster Plantation to live on a vast estate that at one time reached over ten thousand acres. The castle was built but the next Agnew to own Kilwaughter, William, spent little time there, preferring to live in Paris. On his death, he left the estate to his niece, who was married to an Italian aristocrat, and had no intention of living at Kilwaughter.

The castle fell into disrepair in the early twentieth century, and during World War II, Kilwaughter Castle was declared Enemy Property because its owners lived in Italy. After the war, the castle was sold to a scrap dealer, who stripped it of its valuable fittings, including the lead roof. Open to the elements, the castle building quickly fell into ruin.

Kinbane Castle

81 WHITEPARK ROAD, BALLYCASTLE, COUNTY ANTRIM
www.discovernorthernireland.com/kinbane-castle

Set on a limestone headland jutting out to sea, Kinbane
Castle is now in ruins, but visitors who brave the pathway
that leads down to the shoreline and up again to the castle
can enjoy spectacular views and wonder at the lives lived
here in sixteenth-century Ireland. Kinbane was built in
1547 by Colla MacDonnell, son of Lord of Islay and Kintyre,
and part of a powerful clan of Scots chieftains who
migrated to Ireland in the early part of the sixteenth
century, eventually controlling much of the Antrim coast.

In 1551 the castle was besieged by English forces
determined to quash the MacDonnells and four years later
the English returned, this time with cannons. The castle
was partially destroyed and then rebuilt. Colla MacDonnell
died there in 1558 of unknown causes and the castle later
was passed on to his brother, Sorley Boy McDonnell,
an astute leader who spent several years frustrating the
efforts of the English to colonize Ulster with English
settlers, while making strategic alliances with local clans.
At last he obtained a grant to himself and his heirs of
the greater part of the northern Antrim coast, known as
Route country, between the rivers Bann and Bush.

King John's Castle

NICHOLAS STREET, LIMERICK

+353 61 360 788 | *www.kingjohnscastle.com*

Built on the orders of King John of England c. 1210, the castle which still bears his name was constructed on an island in Limerick city that had been a stronghold of the Vikings for several centuries before. The castle was necessary to secure the area for the Anglo-Normans, who had arrived in Ireland some years previously. It is one of the best-preserved Norman castles in Europe, originally with four bastions, three of which survive today, and stands impressively on the river Shannon in a key strategic position.

The castle was at the centre of several sieges at important points in Irish history. Oliver Cromwell's forces, after taking control of the east of Ireland, moved to Limerick in 1650 and 1651, when they besieged the castle. It withstood all attacks but was eventually surrendered due to hunger and disease of the occupants.

The castle was also the scene for the final acts of the war between William of Orange and King James of England. The castle was once again surrendered, this time under the Treaty of Limerick.

King John's Castle has been extensively refurbished in recent years and now houses a visitor centre.

Knappogue Castle

QUIN ROAD, KNOPOGE, ENNIS, COUNTY CLARE
+353 61 360788 | *www.knappoguecastle.ie*

A picturesque tower house with a castellated mansion attached, Knappogue is now a venue for medieval-style banquets. It was built in 1467 by Sean MacNamara, son of Sioda MacNamara. The castle has survived and thrived through its different owners. Owned by the MacNamaras, Earls of Clancullen during Oliver Cromwell's conquest, Knappogue was confiscated and used as a garrison, before being granted to one of Cromwell's soldiers, Arthur Smith, who took up residence there. However, after Charles II was restored to the throne, the castle was handed back to the MacNamaras, who had supported the Royalist cause.

The family held Knappogue until 1800, when it was sold to the Scott family, who invested heavily in restoring the castle but sold it on in 1855 to the Dunboyne family.

During the 1920s the castle was abandoned and the land leased to a local farmer, who was eventually awarded the castle.

The last occupants of the castle were the Andrews family from Houston in Texas, who purchased the property in 1966 and fully restored the castle before selling it back to the Irish government.

Knockdrin Castle

NEAR MULLINGAR, COUNTY WESTMEATH

This imposing Gothic Revival castle dates from around 1830, when it was built for Sir William Levinge MP. Levinge was well placed to acquire some land himself and he bought the twelve thousand acres Knockdrin estate from the Tuite family, who had owned it since Norman times.

Full of Gothic flourishes, Knockdrin is credited to the architect James Shiel, assistant to Francis Johnston, one of Ireland's best-known Gothic Revival architects.

During World War II, a period known in Ireland as The Emergency, Knockdrin was occupied by the Irish Army. In 1945 the castle was restored to the Levinge family, but it was later sold, and then sold on again in the 1960s to a German family, the von Prondzynskis, who own it to this day.

Kylemore Abbey

KYLEMORE ABBEY, POLLACAPPUL, CONNEMARA,
COUNTY GALWAY

+353 95 52001 | *www.kylemoreabbey.com*

Set against a majestic backdrop of woodland and mountains,
with Kylemore Lough spread out below and Connemara's
Twelve Ben mountains in the distance, Kylemore Abbey
dates from the 1860s, when it was built for Mitchell Henry,
a wealthy Liverpool merchant and MP. The Henry family
had many happy years here, but eventually sold
Kylemore to William Montague, the Duke of Manchester,
and his American heiress wife, Helena Zimmerman.
The Manchesters renovated extensively and lived a lavish
lifestyle financed by the duchess's fortune, but in 1921
the house was sold to the Benedictine order of nuns,
who established a boarding school there. Kylemore is
now partnered with Notre Dame University in Indiana,
which uses it as a summer venue for art students.

Lambay Castle

LAMBAY ISLAND, RUSH, COUNTY DUBLIN, K56 KP28
www.lambayisland.ie/castle

An old medieval fort dating back to the sixteenth century, the castle on Lambay Island, the largest island off the east coast of Ireland, was originally built to protect against invasions. When New York banker Cecil Baring (later Baron Revelstoke III) and his wife Maude bought the island in 1904, they commissioned the Anglo-Irish architect Sir Edwin Lutyens to extend and transform the castle. The Lutyens wing was completed in 1910, as well as a rampart wall encircling the castle, and the "White House", a single-storey horseshoe-shaped house. The island, now owned by the Revelstoke Trust, is a self-sufficient natural paradise powered by green energy and fed by a natural spring. Day trips, tours and a variety of courses and retreats can be booked online.

Leamaneh Castle

LEAMANEH NORTH, COUNTY CLARE
www.discoverireland.ie

Situated proudly on the edge of the Burren in County Clare
sits the ruin of Leamaneh Castle, built as a tower house
c. 1480 by a member of the O'Brien clan. The most
infamous of this clan was Red Mary MacMahon, wife of
Conor O'Brien, who added a mansion to the tower house
and resided magnificently in the castle in the seventeenth
century. With red hair and a fiery temper to match, she
was said to have treated servants who displeased her with
all sorts of cruelties. Her husband was mortally wounded
in battles with Cromwell's forces, after which Red Mary,
to save her lands, offered to marry whichever of Cromwell's
officers would choose her. The unfortunate officer who
did was reputed to have died from a kick in the stomach
by Red Mary during an argument. The castle fell into
ruin at the end of the eighteenth century.

Leap Castle

COOLDERRY, COUNTY OFFALY
+353 86 869 0547 | *www.leapcastle.net*

Leap Castle is said to be one of the most haunted houses in Ireland, and is thought to have been built before 1514 by the O'Bannon clan. The current structure was probably built over an older castle. The castle has a square appearance, but it was modernized in the sixteenth century by two-storey one-bay wings that had battlements, Georgian Gothic windows, and a Gothicized Venetian doorway.

Leap Castle was in the O'Carroll family until it was captured in 1642 by John Darby, an English soldier from Oliver Cromwell's army. The Darbys did a large amount of remodelling, and it remained their home until it was looted and burned to a ruin during the uprising in 1922.

Lismore Castle

LISMORE COUNTY, WATERFORD
+353 58 54061 | *www.lismorecastle.com*

Lismore Castle boasts what are said to be the oldest continually cultivated gardens in Ireland, which are seasonally open to visitors. It was originally built in 1185 by soon-to-be King John, who then passed it on to the Bishops of Lismore and from there it was granted to Sir Walter Raleigh.

Richard Boyle subsequently bought the castle and its 42,000 acres for £1500. He rebuilt the castle as a home, adding three-storey gabled ranges around the castle courtyard, a fortified wall, and the upper walled garden around 1605.

Lismore passed on to the Duke of Devonshire and the Cavendish family in 1753, when the fourth duke married the heiress of the Earl of Cork, Lady Charlotte Boyle. The sixth duke worked on extensive restoration of the castle with architects Joseph Paxton and Augustus Pugin in the nineteenth century.

Lohort Castle

CECILSTOWN, COUNTY CORK

Around eight hundred years old, Lohort Castle near Cecilstown, County Cork, has a hazy history. It is an impressively large house at five storeys tall and more than one hundred acres in surrounding land. There is a machicolated parapet around the top storey that remains unbroken, apart from a small section on the eastern side. A distinctive feature is the curved external walls, ten feet wide at the bottom and six feet at the top.

After damage during the civil war and by Cromwell's forces, it was restored around 1750 by the second Earl of Egmont, who included a library and an armoury in the rework, and remodelled in 1876, and yet more additions in the late 19th century. The castle was burned by the Irish Republican Army in 1922 during the War of Independence. It was sold in 2011 but remains unrestored.

Luggala Lodge

ROUNDWOOD, COUNTY WICKLOW

Not strictly a castle but something of a little kingdom, Luggala Lodge was built in 1787 for the La Touches, a Dublin family of Huguenot origin and founders of the Bank of Ireland. The Gothic touches were added later, giving this modest former hunting lodge a fairytale look, which suits its remarkable setting overlooking Lough Tay, within 5000 acres of woods and rocky wilderness.

In 1937, Ernest Guinness of the famous brewing family bought Luggala and gave it as a wedding present to his daughter, Oonagh Guinness. Her parties at Luggala were legendary.

Luggala was inherited by Oonagh's son, Garech Browne, who carried on his mother's tradition of lavish hospitality. An important patron of the arts, he lived part of each year at Luggala until his death in 2018. The estate has recently been sold.

Luttrellstown Castle

CASTLEKNOCK, DUBLIN 15, D15 RH92
+353 1 86 09 600 | www.luttrellstowncastle.com

On the outskirts of Dublin, within the area of English control in Ireland during the Middle Ages called "The Pale", sits Luttrellstown Castle on lands granted to Sir Geoffrey de Luterel by King John of England c. 1210. The castle was built in the fifteenth century by his descendant Geoffrey, who had Anglicized the family name to Luttrell. A later descendant, Colonel Henry Luttrell, switched the loyalty of his regiment during the Jacobite wars in Ireland, aiding the victory of William of Orange, and was later assassinated in his sedan chair in Dublin. Later members of the family were also disliked by Irish nationalists, especially for their role in suppressing the rebellion of 1798, after which the castle was sold to the self-made millionaire publisher Luke White. He changed the castle's name to Woodlands to try to avoid the negativity of the Luttrell name, and added considerably to the castle, including much of the Gothic embellishment seen today. His descendants revived the castle's original name, and subsequent purchasers added much to the decoration of the castle, including the Guinness family and, most recently, J. P. McManus and John Magnier. In 2007 the castle and its golf course were very substantially refurbished, and the castle, with its twelve luxury bedrooms, is available to rent for functions, the most famous being the wedding of David Beckham and Victoria Adams.

Lynch's Castle

SHOP STREET, GALWAY | *www.galwaytourism.ie*

Started in the fourteenth century and added to considerably in the sixteenth century, Lynch's Castle, now in the middle of Shop Street in Galway city, is a four-storey medieval town castle. It was built by the Lynch, originally "De Linch", family (from whom is it said the word "lynching" originated), who were descended from the Anglo-Normans who invaded Ireland from the twelfth century onwards. Galway, from medieval times and centuries afterwards, was ruled by fourteen powerful "tribes" or merchant families, all of Norman descent or Normanized, of whom the Lynches were among the most powerful. Their influence decreased after the Cromwellian conquest of Ireland and after the loss of the Jacobite wars, in which they supported James II against William of Orange. Lynch's Castle is now a branch of a bank, which has supported much restoration work. During opening hours some of the interior can be viewed, but the exterior, with splendid masonry, gargoyles, and the coat of arms of Henry VII of England, can be seen at any time.

Macroom Castle

MACROOM, COUNTY CORK

+353 26 23523 | *www.discoveringcork.ie/macroom-castle*

Many of Ireland's ancient castles have a violent past and Macroom Castle is no different, having been burned down on no less than five occasions. All that remains today is a castellated entrance, walls, and a tower, which nonetheless dominate the centre of the town. Macroom was gifted by Oliver Cromwell to Sir William Penn, father of William Penn of Pennsylvania.

The castle passed through several families, who added to it at different times, but the structure was burned down in 1922. It remained in ruins until the 1960s, when it was substantially demolished. The last owner of the castle gave it to the government for the enjoyment of people of Macroom.

Malahide Castle

MALAHIDE DEMESNE, MALAHIDE, COUNTY DUBLIN
+353 1 816 9538 | *www.malahidecastlesandgardens.ie*

A beautifully preserved medieval castle on the outskirts of Dublin, Malahide Castle is considered to be one of the finest castles in the land, with the added distinction of having been home to the same family, the Talbots, for nearly eight hundred years. The estate began in 1185, when Richard Talbot, a knight who accompanied Henry II of England to Ireland in 1174, was granted the "lands and harbour of Malahide". The castle was home to the Talbots from then until 1976, except for a brief interlude during Cromwell's invasion in 1649. The building was enlarged in the reign of Edward IV of England, and the towers added in 1765. Dublin County Council bought the 265-acre property in 1975, allowing the public access to its fine interior and superb gardens.

Mallow Castle

CASTLELANDS, MALLOW, COUNTY CORK
+353 22 42222 | *www.mallow.ie*

Mallow Castle is in fact two castles. One is the remains of a sixteenth-century fortification and castellated manor house. There are remains too of a far earlier fortification held by the Norman de Rupe, or de Roche family.

In the 1580s or early 1590s, it was taken over by Sir John Norreys, who had been appointed Lord President of Munster by Queen Elizabeth I of England and gifted six thousand acres of surrounding land. Thomas Norreys' daughter Elizabeth was the godchild of the queen, who gifted her a small herd of white deer, the descendants of which can still be seen today. The young Elizabeth was married to Sir John Jephson, and the Jephson family held Mallow Castle for almost four hundred years, building a new mansion on the estate, following a fire during the Williamite War. The Jephson family held the seat until 1984, when they sold it to an American millionaire.

Manderley Castle

VICTORIA ROAD, KILLINEY, COUNTY DUBLIN

Formerly known as Ayesha Castle and Victoria Castle, Manderley is a large castellated mansion in a dreamy setting overlooking Killiney Bay, about ten miles south of Dublin city.

The castle was built in 1940 by a property developer, Robert Warren, who had made his fortune selling off plots of land alongside the developing railway line which brought affluent Dubliners to the seaside. They named the castle Victoria Castle in honour of the new British queen, who acceded to the throne in 1840. The castle was ravaged by fire in the 1920s and was later bought by the whiskey magnate Sir Thomas Talbot Power, who renovated it at great expense and renamed it Ayesha, after H. Rider Haggard's sorceress, the original "She-who-must-be-obeyed" in his 1887 blockbuster novel *She*. The castle is now the private home of Irish musician Enya, who has renamed it Manderley.

Manorhamilton Castle

6 CASTLE STREET, MANORHAMILTON, COUNTY LEITRIM, F91 HY88

+353 71 985 5249 | *www.leitrimtourism.com*

The ruins of Manorhamilton Castle dominate the village of the same name. Both were built by Scottish settler and soldier Sir Frederick Hamilton, who, around 1622, was granted land in County Leitrim. He and his well-connected wife (her father was a member of the Privy Council for Ireland) amassed an estate of some 18,000 acres, much of which had been seized from the O'Rourke family. The Hamiltons established a town and built the castle around 1634, but Hamilton was often absent, spending some time in Germany with the Swedish army. Later he retired to Scotland, and Manorhamilton Castle was attacked by the army of Ulick Burke, the Catholic leader of the Royalist army in Ireland. The castle never recovered and fell into ruin.

Markree Castle

COLLOONEY, COUNTY SLIGO

+353 71 916 7800 | *www.markreecastle.ie*

Ancestral home of the Cooper family, Markree Castle is a handsome eighteenth-century castellated house standing on the site of an original seventeenth-century dwelling. The castellated entrances to the estate were built in the 1830s to the design of Francis Goodwin of London. Mrs Alexander, the hymn writer, stayed at Markree and it's said that the line "The rich man in his castle" in "All Things Bright and Beautiful" is a reference to Markree. The castle is now run as a small hotel.

Maudlin Castle

30 MAUDLIN STREET, HIGHHAYS, KILKENNY, R95 Y8NE

Maudlin Castle is a sixteenth-century tower house that once formed part of the town's defences and also acted as a grain store for Kilkenny Castle. There is evidence of an earlier structure that may once have been a hospital, possibly as early as the late thirteenth century.

The name Maudlin is derived from the Irish for Magdalen. Many leper hospitals were dedicated to St Mary Magdalene. It became a hospital of sorts again in 1598, when the Corporation of Kilkenny leased the castle to a merchant of the town "reserving the use of the best chamber thereof for such as shall be infected of the 'dyseas commonly called Leprosie'".

Maynooth Castle

MAIN STREET, MAYNOOTH, COUNTY KILDARE
+353 1 628 6744 | *www.heritageireland.ie*

Once known as one of the richest castles in Ireland, Maynooth Castle was home to the Fitzgeralds, who would later become the Earls of Kildare. The original castle keep, built at the beginning of the thirteenth century, became a residence for the Lord Deputies of Ireland, but by the seventeenth century the building was decaying, and it now lies in ruins. It stands as the entrance to Maynooth University, which was founded in 1795 and which became famous for the education of the Irish Catholic priests.

McDermott's Castle

A majestic castle set on a half-acre island in Lough Key in County Roscommon, McDermott's Castle's foundations date from the twelfth century. What appears to have been an important castle was in fact designed as a folly by the architect John Nash and built on the island to provide a romantic outlook for the Rockingham mansion on the shores of Lough Key. It was destroyed by fire in the 1950s, and the castle was also partially destroyed in the 1940s. The poet W. B. Yeats visited Castle Island in 1890 and considered setting up an artistic centre there.

Menlo Castle

MENLO, COUNTY GALWAY

+353 91 536 547 | *www.galwaytourism.ie*

The ancestral seat of the Blake family, a prominent Catholic family and one of the fourteen Tribes of Galway, Menlo Castle has a stunning setting on the banks of Lough Corrib, outside Galway city. Its ruined walls are now engulfed in ivy but at one time the castle, parts of which date from the sixteenth century, was famous for its hospitality and for its annual "Maying in Menlo" festival when tenants from miles around were invited to a garden party in the grounds. The Blakes lived at Menlo from 1600 to 1910, when the house was tragically destroyed by a fire that took the life of an invalid daughter of the house and of a young housemaid.

As an aside, California's Menlo Park, in the heart of Silicon Valley, was founded by two Galway immigrants and named after the area's Menlo Castle.

Minard Castle

ANNASCAUL, DINGLE PENINSULA, COUNTY KERRY

Eagle-eyed film buffs might recognize Minard Castle from David Lean's 1969 film *Ryan's Daughter*, filmed here and at other locations on the Dingle Peninsula. The ruined fortress sits atop a hill above a boulder-strewn beach. The castle dates back to the sixteenth century, when it was built as a stronghold for the Knights of Kerry. In 1650 it was partially destroyed by Cromwell's army and all inside perished.

Beyond the castle, a side path leads to the spring of Tobar Eoin, or St John's Well, whose waters allegedly hold a cure for eyesight problems. Above the well a tree is festooned with strips of rag, each tied there for a wish or a prayer.

Moher Tower

The Cliffs of Moher attract huge numbers of tourists
(over 1.5 million visitors annually), so it can get crowded
there at peak times. But make your way to Moher Tower
at the furthermost tip of the cliffs and you'll be rewarded
with peace and quiet to enjoy the dramatic setting. Built
as a watchtower during the Napoleonic Wars (1803–15),
Moher Tower sits on a wild headland called Hag's Head,
with stunning views that take in the Aran Islands and
Galway Bay, as well as Loop Head and the Dingle Peninsula.

The Gaelic word *Mothar* means "ruined fort", and a
first-century BC fort stood where Moher Tower now
stands. No trace remains of this two-thousand-year-old
fort, but the Napoleonic tower provides a great backdrop
for photographs.

In season, the location is served by the Cliffs of Moher
Shuttle Bus.

Monea Castle

ENNISKILLEN, BT74 8EQ

+44 28 9082 3207 | *www.discovernorthernireland.com/Monea-Castle-Enniskillen-P2902*

Open to the elements and to the public, Monea Castle is a large, well-preserved structure that was built in 1618 for Malcolm Hamilton. The castle follows the traditional castle and bawn style, with the bawn being a walled enclosure.

In the Irish Rebellion of 1641, the castle was attacked by Rory Maguire, who "slew and murthered eight Protestants" here. In 1688 it was occupied by Gustav Hamilton, the Governor of Enniskillen, whose family held the estate until the early 1700s. A few decades later the castle was destroyed by fire and subsequently abandoned.

Mongavlin Castle

SAINT JOHNSTON, COUNTY DONEGAL

Located a few miles from the village of Saint Johnston on the banks of the river Foyle stand the ruins of Mongavlin Castle, the one-time stronghold of the O'Donnell clan. In the sixteenth century the castle was home to the Scottish princess, Ineen Dubh, daughter of James MacDonnell, Lord of the Isles, and mother of the famous fighting prince, Red Hugh O'Donnell. It's said that Ineen came to Ireland with a band of fifty to one hundred strong men, most of them called Crawford, and some of their descendants are still living in this part of Donegal. Mongavlin was granted, along with 1000 acres, to the Scottish lord, Ludovic Stewart, second Duke of Lennox, in 1610, and his family held it for generations before it fell into ruins.

Monkstown Castle

MONKSTOWN, COUNTY DUBLIN

Set in the fashionable Dublin suburb of Monsktown and surrounded by housing, the remains of Monkstown Castle and its gardens provide an oasis of calm close to a busy roundabout. In medieval times, the castle was the centre of a farm owned by the Cistercian monks of St Mary's Abbey. When the abbey was dissolved in 1540, the castle was granted to John Travers, who came to Ireland from Cornwall later, during Cromwell's time.

Today the castle is mostly in ruins but the enclosed garden is well maintained and can be visited.

Mountgarrett Castle

MOUNT GARRETT BRIDGE, COUNTY KILKENNY

The ruined remains of a castle overlooking New Ross was once the residence of Patrick Barrett, Lord Chancellor of Ireland and Bishop of Ferns, who rebuilt it at the beginning of the fifteenth century. It later passed through several families, notably the Butlers, who were granted the title Viscount Mountgarrett in 1550 by Henry VIII. It was briefly confiscated during Cromwell's time but restored to the Mountgarretts, who held it until the twelfth viscount died without heir in 1793.

Moygara Castle

COUNTY SLIGO

+353 86 608 3753 | *www.moygaracastle.com*

Legend has it that a pot of gold is buried under the ground at Moygara Castle but, like many an Irish pot of gold, it has never been found. The castle, which consists of a large square bawn with a tower at each of its four corners, was built in the late sixteenth and early seventeenth centuries, but there's evidence too of an earlier tower house along the northern side of the bawn wall. The castle served as the centre of the late medieval O'Gara Lordship of Coolavin, who controlled much of the area.

Moyode Castle

ATHENRY, COUNTY GALWAY

A sixteenth-century fortified tower house originally built for the Burke family, Moyode Castle sits in peaceful countryside about 3.5 miles from the Galway market town of Athenry.

Members of the landowning Persse family owned the Moyode estate for generations and built an alternative on their land in the 1820s. They were known for their sporting pursuits and also for their poor treatment of tenants during the famine. The family left Moyode altogether three decades before the house was burned in 1922. The original tower was purchased as a ruin by the American historian James Charles Roy in 1969, and the tower has been largely restored.

Muckross House

KILLARNEY NATIONAL PARK, MUCKROSS, KILLARNEY,
COUNTY KERRY, V93 CK73
+353 64 667 0144 | www.muckross-house.ie

A grand Gothic-style mansion in a magical setting overlooking the Lakes of Killarney, Muckross House was built by the Herbert family, who prospered during the eighteenth century, thanks to copper mining on the Muckross Peninsula. They built Muckross in the 1840s and continued to upgrade it over many years, in the hope that their distant relative, Queen Victoria, would come to visit them in Killarney. She finally did come to stay in 1861. Her visit caused them to spend a fortune on upgrading the 65-room house and gardens.

After the Herberts ran into financial difficulties, Muckross was sold in 1899 to Arthur Guinness, first Baron Ardilaun, who rented it out to wealthy tourists. It was later sold to a Californian mining magnate, whose family donated it to the Irish nation in 1932, along with 11,000 acres. When the house and lands were gifted to the State in 1924, this created the first national park in Ireland.

Narrow Water Castle

67 NEWRY ROAD, WARRENPOINT, NEWRY,
COUNTY DOWN, BT34 3LE
+44 28 9082 3207

Built on the banks of the Clanryle river, close to the point where it enters Carlingford Lough, Narrow Water Castle dates from the 1560s. It replaced an earlier fortress built by Hugh de Lacy, first Earl of Ulster, to stop enemy boats making their way upriver to towards the town of Newry.

By 1580 the castle was held by Hugh Magennis, Chief of the Mournes, but skirmishes with the English forces saw it taken and granted back again to the Magennis family, who managed to hold it for almost a century, before it was confiscated once more. This time it was sold to the Hall family, wealthy landowners who developed the nearby port and town of Warrenpoint and who, around the 1690s, built themselves an alternative home, Mount Hall, on higher ground than the tower house. Mount Hall was later incorporated into a grand castle, which was begun around 1817 and was built in the fashionable Gothic Revival style of the day.

Meanwhile the riverside castle languished, having been used variously as a saltworks and a dog kennels.

The estate remains in the Hall family today, though the tower house was given over to the State in the 1950s and is now a tourist attraction.

Nenagh Castle

O'RAHILLY STREET, NENAGH, COUNTY TIPPERARY

+353 67 33850 | *www.nenagh.ie*

The castle at Nenagh must once have been an awe-inspiring sight, with its five towers surrounding a courtyard. Now all that remains of the thirteenth-century complex are fragments of the walls, and a single tower, dubbed Nenagh Round by locals. Nenagh Castle was started by Theobald Fitzwalter Butler, and was completed by his son, also Theobald, in about 1220. The Butlers later became Earls of Ormond and Nenagh remained their principal seat until 1391, when the family moved to Kilkenny Castle.

It was here, in 1336, that a peace treaty was signed between James Butler, first Earl of Ormonde, and a representative of the Irish O'Kennedy clan. Six hundred years later, the original treaty was presented as a gift to US President John F. Kennedy, during a State visit to Ireland in 1963, and is now on view in the JFK Library in Massachusetts.

Situated in the centre of the town surrounded by its own park, Nenagh Round has become a popular tourist attraction. The renovated tower is around 100 feet tall and has a base of around 55 feet. Inside, there is a stone spiral staircase of 101 steps to the top.

Newtown Castle

NEWTOWN, COUNTY CLARE

+353 65 707 7200 | *www.newtowncastle.com*

Located on the Burren Way, a walk through the stunning Burren limestone landscape, Newtown Castle rises up from a unique pyramid-style base that has been likened to a rocket launcher.

The sixteenth-century cylindrical tower house has several defensive features, such as narrow slit windows, gun loops, and murder holes. Most notable is the steeply pitched roof, complete with parapet walk. Once owned by the O'Brien clan, it later passed to the O'Loughlins, who remained there until the 1800s when it was abandoned and fell into ruin.

Carefully restored, the castle has a number of notable features, such as domed wattled ceilings, and a remarkable conical ceiling, created using seven tons of Irish oak. The four windows below provide far-reaching views of the Burren landscape and Galway Bay.

Newtown Castle is part of the Burren College of Art, which regularly uses it as an exhibition space.

O'Brien's Tower

BURREN WAY, LISLORKAN NORTH, COUNTY CLARE

+353 83 830 2523

O'Brien's Tower is a rare kind of Irish tower house that, for once, does not come with a troubled history of warring clans and confiscation. Rather, it was built, not as a fortification, but as a viewing point for tourists on a stunning location at the Cliffs of Moher.

The tower was the brainchild of Cornelius O'Brien, a landowner with vast holdings in County Clare, who was also MP for the county. A benign landlord who ensured his tenants lived in habitable dwellings, O'Brien initiated a number of building projects to create employment and improve the countryside. He built two schools and an important bridge, and carried out numerous improvements to his own estate, called Birchfield.

Built in 1835, the tower was an instant hit with visitors who had begun to flock to cliffs. It became a magnet for artists and photographers and, nowadays, for adventurous selfie takers. The best views from the tower are of the cliffs themselves but visitors might also catch a glimpse of the Aran Islands, mist allowing.

O'Malley Castle

CLARE ISLAND, COUNTY MAYO | *www.clareisland.ie*

Dominating Clare Island harbour, Clare Island Castle is often referred to as O'Malley Castle, after its most famous occupant, the Pirate Queen Grace O'Malley (Granuaile), an Irish folk hero of legendary status, who at one time controlled much of the coast of the west of Ireland. Although Granuaile had several castles at her disposal, she was particularly fond of the keep on Clare Island, with its narrow windows commanding strategic views of Clew Bay.

Granuaile was a trader who sold tallow and wool to the continent, but she also captured ships that strayed into her sea kingdom off the west coast of Ireland. She fought off incursions by the English and at one point sailed to England and up the river Thames to meet with Queen Elizabeth I to put her case. There is little in the records about what was said at the meeting, except a note that the women chatted in Latin, as O'Malley didn't speak English and the queen had no Irish.

Granuaile lived on Clare Island and loved island life. She died in 1603 and her body was entombed in a twelfth-century Cistercian church on the island, which is now in ruins.

Oranmore Castle

CASTLE ROAD, INNPLOT, ORANMORE, COUNTY GALWAY
+353 86 600 3160 | *www.oranmorecastle.com*

A romantic stronghold on the edge of Galway Bay, Oranmore Castle was built during the fifteenth century, most likely on the site of an older castle. It became a base for the Clanricardes, a prominent Norman family of Galway, but the castle later passed to the Blakes, who traced their lineage back to the fourteen Tribes of Galway.

The castle played an important role in the defence of Galway during the Confederate Rebellion in the 1640s: provisions were shipped from the castle to the besieged city. However at some stage it was abandoned and fell into ruins in the 1800s. In the 1940s it was bought for £200 by cousin of Winston Churchill, who then gave it to her daughter, the writer Anita Leslie. She renovated the castle and settled there with her husband Bill King, who was believed to have been the only surviving submarine commander from the Second World War.

In 1967, King set out to sail the world in a boat he had built himself. The two-masted Galway Blazer II twice failed to circumnavigate the world, but he eventually succeeded in sailing single-handedly around the world in 1970.

The castle is now occupied by artist Leonie King (daughter of Anita Leslie and Bill King) and her husband Alec Finn of the music band De Dannan.

Ormond Castle

6 CASTLE STREET, CARRICKBEG, CARRICK-ON-SUIR,
COUNTY TIPPERARY

+353 51 640 787 | *www.herageireland.ie*

When Queen Elizabeth I took the throne in 1558, she appointed Thomas Butler, tenth Earl of Ormond and her childhood friend, as Lord Treasurer of Ireland, making him Privy Councillor, and excusing him of all his debts.

Secure in his connections, Thomas set about improving the family seat, Ormond Castle, in the town of Carrick-on-Suir. The castle was, in fact, built over two centuries by the Butlers, one of the great Anglo-Norman clans. Thomas wanted a castle to impress, rather than to defend, and he followed the Elizabethan style closely, creating an imposing manor house of many windows, with a grand Long Gallery within, hung with tapestries and decorated with plaster friezes.

Parkes Castle

KILMORE, FIVEMILEBOURNE, COUNTY LEITRIM, F91 FP71

+353 71 916 4149 | *www.parkescastle.com*

Set in Ireland's Lake District, on the shores of Lough Gill, Parkes Castle was once the stronghold of clan chief Brian O'Rourke, who had the misfortune to take in a survivor of a Spanish Armada ship that had sunk in the bay. For this, he was deemed a traitor, and was captured and hanged at Tyburn, London, in 1591. His confiscated estate was sold to a planter, Roger Parke, around 1610. Parke kept the walls of the original bawn and demolished the existing tower, using the stones to build a three-storey manor on the eastern side, adorning it with mullioned windows and tall chimneys.

Parkes Castle has been restored in recent years to give a flavour of castle life in the seventeenth century.

Portaferry Castle

PORTAFERRY, NEWTOWNARDS, BT22 1NY

+44 28 9082 3214 | *www.visitardsandnorthdown.com*

Portaferry Castle is a sixteenth-century tower house strategically positioned on a slope overlooking Portaferry harbour. It's a relatively simple structure, square in plan with one projecting tower to the south, where a turret rises an extra storey and contains the entrance and stair from ground floor to first floor.

The entrance is protected by a machicolation above, with a murder hole in the ceiling of the entrance chamber for added protection. There isn't a whole lot to see: in the words of the archaeologist Robert M. Chapple, "these days, the ivy and weed strewn battlements make excellent perches for gulls looking stoically out to sea, while the simple ruins can still hold the fascination of children and adults, imagining imminent attack by land and sea". In other words, it's worth a visit.

Across from the village of Portaferry, on the other side of the mouth of Strangford Lough, lies the village of Strangford, with Strangford Castle.

Portumna Castle

PORTUMNA, COUNTY GALWAY H53 YK27

+353 90 974 1658 | *www.heritageireland.ie/en/west/ portumnacastleandgardens*

A large symmetrical three-storey building with elegant corner towers and a Jacobean-style gabled roof, Portumna Castle was completed around 1618 as the seat of the Burke family. Originally de Burgos, the Burkes became Earls of Clanricarde and were important landowners in County Galway. The castle sits overlooking Lough Derg on the Shannon.

The first owner of Portumna Castle, Richard Burke, or de Burgo, was the fourth Earl of Clanricarde, and was knighted for his efforts at the Battle of Kinsale. He married the widow of the second Earl of Essex, Frances Walsingham, and began to build his castle in Portumna around 1611. It's said to have cost £10,000, and was considered one of the finest homes in Ireland.

The castle continued to be the main residence of the Burkes until it was gutted by fire in the 1820s, and the family later built a new residence close by. This too was destroyed in 1922 and its stones used to build a Roman Catholic church in the nearby town.

Portumna Castle and gardens have been refurbished by Duchas, the Irish heritage body.

Quintin Castle

3 KEARNEY ROAD, PORTAFERRY, NEWTOWNARDS, BT22 1QB

+44 28 42 729215 | *www.quintincastle.co.uk*

Quintin Castle enjoys a spectacular setting on the Ards Peninsula, overlooking the Irish Sea.

Parts of the castle date back to 1184, when it was built by John de Courcy. It was later occupied by the Savage family and their dependants, the Smiths.

In the seventeenth century, the castle had several additions, before the building was sold to George Ross, a landowner who allowed Quintin to fall into ruin. It was restored again in the 1850s by Elizabeth Calvert, a descendant of Ross.

The castle is now owned by the Tayto Group of crisps fame, and is now a venue for weddings and conferences.

Redwood Castle

LORRHA, NEAR NENAGH, COUNTY TIPPERARY
+353 87 747 9566 | *www.tipperary.com*

A popular tourist attraction in north Tipperary, Redwood Castle dates from the early 1200s, when it was built by the Anglo-Norman De Cougan family. More than a century later, the castle was granted to the O'Kennedy clan, who extended upwards, adding three further levels and extra fortifications including a murder hole. Redwood later passed into the possession of the MacEgans, a family that specialized in the practice of Brehon law, and founded a school of law at the castle. The MacEgans held the castle until around 1650, when they were routed by Cromwell's army.

In the 1970s, Michael Egan, a descendant of the original MacEgans, bought the castle and renovated it gradually over the years. It is now open to the public, and tours are provided.

Rockfleet Castle

NEWPORT, COUNTY MAYO

www.destinationwestport.com/places-to-visit/
towns-and-villages/newport/rockfleet-castle

A well-preserved fifteenth- or sixteenth-century tower house situated on an inlet in Clew Bay, Rockfleet was said to have been the principal residence of the pirate queen, Grace O'Malley. Granuaile, as she was also known, was married at the age of fifteen to Donal O'Flaherty, who was heir to the kingdom of Connemara. However, continuous warring with neighbours depleted his resources and it was down to Granuaile to build up their fortunes, which she did by trading in tallow and hides and pirating at sea. After Donal was killed in a skirmish over property, Granuaile married Richard Burke, who owned Rockfleet, and established her own fleet here in 1566. Granuaile lived to an old age. She died in 1603 at Rockfleet Castle and was buried in the Cistercian Abbey on Clare Island.

Roscrea Castle

CASTLE STREET, ROSCREA, COUNTY TIPPERARY, E53 F652
+353 505 21850 | *www.heritageireland.ie*

A carefully restored castle complex with gate tower, drawbridge, curtain walls, and two corner towers, Roscrea Castle has its origins in the thirteenth century, when it was built following the discovery of silver mines nearby. The south-east tower is sometimes known as King John's Castle. Although it dates from after his death, there is evidence that King John ordered a *motam et bretagium* (motte and tower) to be built on the site in 1213 as part of his efforts to solidify his conquest of Ireland, particularly the midlands and southern counties. The castle became the property of the Butlers of Ormond in 1315 and they held it until the eighteenth century. It's another castle with a bloody history: during the wars that culminated in Cromwell's conquest of Ireland, the castle and the town were taken in 1646 by Owen Roe O'Neill and his army, who reportedly killed everyone in the town.

Later, the castle was used as a barracks, a school, a library, and a tuberculosis sanatorium.

In the castle courtyard stands Damer House, a Queen Anne building which now houses a series of exhibitions, including a permanent display of old farm and kitchen implements.

Shane's Castle

RANDALSTOWN, COUNTY ANTRIM

Once known as Edenduffcarrick, Shane's Castle is an intriguing series of ruins on the shores of Antrim Bay. The original castle built here in the seventeenth century took its name from Shane McBrian O'Neill, of the ancient royal Irish family, who famously charmed Elizabeth I into recognizing his fiefdom.

The castle was enlarged in the eighteenth century when battlements were added, and also a long conservatory facing the lake, which was designed by the English architect John Nas and filled with exotic fruit trees. The house grew to include a ballroom, a theatre, and a round room for writing letters. John, first Viscount O'Neill, lived at Shane's Castle during this time and up till his death in 1798.

When the castle burned down in 1816, local lore had it that the resident banshee of the castle (a fairy figure who heralds the death of a family member) had caused the fire, displeased that her space had been taken during a very large house party. It's more likely that a rook's nest in a chimney caught fire. A later castle built in Victorian times was also burned, and a modern house was built on the grounds.

The grounds are now open to the public, and the conservatory, having been restored, is now a camellia house.

Slade Castle

A well-preserved castle that dominates the tiny fishing village of Slade on the Hook Peninsula in County Wexford, Slade Castle was most likely built by the Laffan family, who were among the first colonists to arrive in Ireland after Strongbow's invasion of 1169. The Laffans were prosperous merchants who ensconced themselves at Slade Castle in the late 1400s and, in time, enlarged the five-storey castle with a two-storey fortification, complete with murder hole.

The Laffans would have enjoyed sweeping views of the sea and nearby Bannow Bay, where the Normans first landed in 1169. The castle changed hands in the seventeenth century and later was used as a storehouse for a nearby saltworks. By the nineteenth century, it had been converted into a tenement housing three families.

The castle was taken into State ownership in the 1940s and renovated.

Slane Castle

SLANE, COUNTY MEATH

+353 41 988 4477 | *www.slanecastle.ie*

Slane Castle overlooks the river Boyne, in an area of Ireland rich in history. The name Slane comes from the Irish *Baile Shláine*, meaning the Town of Sláine mac Dela, the son of the legendary first High King of Ireland. The original land and castle on the site were owned by the Anglo-Norman Flanders (now Fleming) family, who supported the Jacobite cause, which was dealt a serious blow in that famous battle. After this, the Flemings' land was confiscated and purchased by the Conyngham family from Donegal; a descendant still owns the property. The Conynghams significantly reconstructed the castle in 1785 and laid out the adjoining village of Slane in the style of a model British village.

The castle has become newsworthy in recent decades due to its hosting of rock concerts in the natural grassy amphitheatre on its grounds, which can hold 80,000 people. Starting in 1981, the castle has hosted concerts by many famous Irish and international bands.

The castle is open for tours, which can include the recently opened Slane Whiskey Distillery on the grounds. It can also be hired for weddings and other events.

Smarmore Castle

ARDEE, COUNTY LOUTH | +353 4 986 5080

A medieval castle now occupies the centre of a much larger building, with Georgian-era additions on either side. For centuries, the castle was occupied by the Taaffe family, later Earls of Carlingford, who are thought to have settled in Ireland from Wales around 1196, and who were granted vast estates in Louth, Cork, Longford, Waterford, Mayo, Meath, Westmeath, and Tipperary, under Queen Elizabeth I and King James I. Male Taaffes distinguished themselves in battle across Europe and rose to high-ranking positions, particularly in Austria, where the family were created counts.

The family line died out in the 1960s with Edward Charles Richard Taaffe, an Austrian gemologist who discovered the rare mineral, taaffeite. Upon his death in 1967, no heir remained, which rendered both the Austrian and Irish titles extinct.

Smarmore Castle was more recently run as a hotel and leisure centre, but it has now been converted into an addiction clinic.

Strancally Castle

Overlooking the river Blackwater, Strancally Castle was designed and built around 1830 by James and George Pain for John Kiely, MP for Clonmel and High Sheriff of County Waterford.

The castle was later owned by the wealthy Anglo-Irish Whitelock Lloyd family, the most distinguished member of which was William Whitelock Lloyd, an army officer who befriended Oscar Wilde at Oxford and who fought in the Anglo-Zulu war in South Africa in 1878. His scores of sketches of the conflict and the Zulu landscape were collected long after his death in a book, *A Soldier-Artist in Zululand*, with a foreword by Prince Charles.

Near the castle is old Strancally Castle, which lies hidden in the trees at the water's edge. It was built for Raymond le Gros, a cousin of Norman invader Strongbow, in the twelfth century. By the sixteenth century, the castle was said to have been occupied by Spaniards, who were said to have lured local landowners to a banquet in the castle and then dropped them through a secret trapdoor into a flooded cave.

Tandragee Castle

TANDRAGEE, COUNTY ARMAGH

The site of Tandragee Castle in County Armagh once belonged to the powerful O'Hanlon clan and later came as a dowry with Millicent Sparrow, who married the sixth Duke of Manchester, Viscount Mandeville. It was entirely rebuilt in the baronial style about 1837 by the duke, who was a staunch Tory and an active promoter of the Protestant cause. It's a handsome building with a solid machicolated tower at one end, while the opposite end has a gabled block somewhat similar to a Tudor manor house.

The family held it until 1939, when the castle was leased to the US Army in preparation for the Second World War. In the 1950s, the castle was sold to the Hutchinson family, who would go on to establish the Tayto brand of potato crisps.

Thomastown Castle

THOMASTOWN, COUNTY TIPPERARY

A picturesque ruin smothered in ivy is all that remains of a seventeenth-century house built by George Mathew, half-brother of the first Duke of Ormond. The building was dramatically altered by Richard Morrison and enlarged in neo-Gothic style in about 1812, with new wings and four slender towers to the front.

Thomastown was the childhood home of Father Theobold Mathew, who established the Teetotal Abstinence Society in 1838, inviting members to take "the pledge" to stay sober for life.

At its height, just before the Great Famine of 1845–8, his movement enrolled some three million people, or more than half of the adult population of Ireland. In 1844, he visited Liverpool, Manchester, and London with almost equal success.

Trim Castle

TRIM, COUNTY MEATH
+353 46 943 8616 | *www.meath.ie*

Trim Castle is the largest and best-preserved Norman castle in Ireland, built over seven acres at a ford over the River Boyne in County Meath, which was navigable from the Irish Sea, about twenty-five miles from the coast. It was started around 1172 by Hugh de Lacy as the centre of administration of his Lordship of Meath. Originally ringed by a wooden palisade, this was attacked and burned by the then High King of Ireland, after which the castle went through various stages of rebuilding in stone over the next few centuries, including the central three-storey keep, which has walls three metres thick. Ownership of the castle passed through many notable families, from the Norman de Lacys and de Grenvilles to the Mortimers, and then the English King Henry IV. It also saw action during Cromwell's campaigns in Ireland and, after the Jacobite wars at the end of the seventeenth century, the castle changed ownership, as so many did, into the Wellesley family, which later produced the Duke of Wellington. Eventually, in 1993, the castle was sold to the Irish State, which has restored it since, opening it to the public in 2000, after it had been used in the making of the film *Braveheart*, starring Mel Gibson, and as a double for various Scottish and English castles in other films. The grounds are open for self-exploration but entry to the keep is by guided tour only.

Tully Castle

LOUGH SHORE ROAD, DERRYGONNELLY, ENNISKILLEN
www.discovernorthernireland.com

Many Irish castles come with a bloody history but the story of Tully Castle is more tragic than most. Built for the Scottish planter, Sir John Hume, in 1619, the handsome hillside fortification overlooking Lough Erne is very impressive, with ample living space, vast kitchen and stores, and a formal garden inside its bawn walls. But during the Irish Rebellion of 1641, local clansman Rory Maguire set out to recapture his family's lands from the planters, and Tully Castle was in his sights. He arrived there on Christmas Eve of that year and found the castle full of women and children. Lady Mary Hume surrendered the castle, in exchange for the safe conduct of all the occupants but instead, on Christmas Day, the Maguires killed over sixty women and children and fifteen men, sparing only the Hume family. The castle was pillaged and burned, and it has remained a ruin to this day.

Tullynally Castle

CASTLEPOLLARD, COUNTY WESTMEATH
+353 44 966 1856 | *www.tullynallycastle.ie*

With its romantic skyline of towers, turrets, battlements, and gateways, Tullynally Castle is said to cover a greater area than any other castellated country house in Ireland. What started as a plain Georgian house was enlarged and extended into a Gothic mansion that was originally called Pakenham Hall House. Further additions in the mid 1800s saw Tullynally's outer offices castellated and joined to the main building, creating the impression of one vast castle. Home to the Pakenham family for the last 350 years, the castle takes its name from the Irish "Tulaigh an Eallaigh" meaning "the hill of the swan", so named because the castle overlooks Lough Derravaragh, the lake from the famous Irish myth "The Children of Lir".